Floating Worlds

The Focus Animation Series aims to provide unique, accessible content that may not otherwise be published. We allow researchers, academics, and professionals the ability to quickly publish high-impact, current literature in the field of animation for a global audience. This series is a fine complement to the existing, robust animation titles available through CRC Press/Focal Press.

Series Editor Giannalberto Bendazzi, currently an independent scholar, is a former Visiting Professor of History of Animation at the Nanyang Technological University in Singapore and a former professor at the Università degli Studi di Milano. We welcome any submissions to help grow the wonderful content we are striving to provide to the animation community: **giannalbertobendazzi@gmail.com**.

Published:

Maria Roberta Novielli; *Floating Worlds: A Short History of Japanese Animation*

Giannalberto Bendazzi; *Twice the First: Quirino Cristiani and the Animated Feature Film*

Forthcoming:

Pamela Taylor Turner; *Infinite Animation: The Life and Work of Adam Beckett*

Lina X. Aguirre; *Experimental Animation in Contemporary Latin America*

Cinzia Bottini; *Redesigning Animation: United Productions of America*

Marco Bellano; *Václav Trojan: Music Composition in Czech Animated Films*

Floating Worlds
A Short History of Japanese Animation

By

Maria Roberta Novielli

CRC Press
Taylor & Francis Group
Boca Raton London New York

CRC Press is an imprint of the
Taylor & Francis Group, an **informa** business

A FOCAL PRESS BOOK

CRC Press
Taylor & Francis Group
6000 Broken Sound Parkway NW, Suite 300
Boca Raton, FL 33487-2742

© 2018 by Taylor & Francis Group, LLC
CRC Press is an imprint of Taylor & Francis Group, an Informa business

No claim to original U.S. Government works

Printed on acid-free paper

International Standard Book Number-13: 978-1-1385-7128-0 (Hardback)

Library of Congress Cataloging-in-Publication Data

Names: Novielli, Maria Roberta, 1964- author.
Title: Floating worlds : a short history of Japanese animation / Maria Roberta Novielli.
Description: Boca Raton : Taylor & Francis, 2018.
Identifiers: LCCN 2017048748 | ISBN 9781138571280 (hardback : alk. paper)
Subjects: LCSH: Animated films--Japan--History and criticism.
Classification: LCC NC1766.J3 N684 2018 | DDC 791.43/340952--dc23
LC record available at https://lccn.loc.gov/2017048748

Visit the Taylor & Francis Web site at
http://www.taylorandfrancis.com

and the CRC Press Web site at
http://www.crcpress.com

It is a wonderful achievement that an accurate history of Japanese animation has been summed up in 2017, a year marking a turning point since it coincides with the centenary of its birth.

The accurate description by Roberta Novielli expands a new perspective for the Japanese people and also provides knowledge of deep interest to people around the world. It is a "must" book for those who are interested in Japanese animation.

Yamamura Kōji

Contents

Foreword

TRANSCRIPTION

The transcription systems are Hepburn for Japanese and Pinyin for Chinese.

Long accents on vowels indicate their lengthening, not doubling.

NAMES OF PERSONS

The names are given according to the Japanese use: first the surname, then the name.

Chronology of the main historical periods is as follows:

Asuka (from late VI century to 710)

Nara (710–794)

Heian (794–1185)

Kamakura (1185–1333)

Kemmu Restoration (1333–1336)

Yoshino or Nanbokuchō (1336–1392)

Ashikaga or Muromachi (1392–1573)

Momoyama or Azuchi Momoyama (1573–1600)

Edo or Tokugawa (1603–1867)

Meiji (1868–1912)

Taishō (1912–1926)

Shōwa (1926–1989)

Heisei (1989–)

Preface

JAPANESE ANIMATION IS ONE of the richest and most interesting artistic forms of the international scene and in 2017 it celebrated its 100th year of existence. The intention of my book is to travel through its development and to analyze its techniques, to investigate the profiles of its protagonists and, above all, to understand the political, economic and cultural background from which every production stems, with cinema being the ideal interpreter of the richness and complexity of society.

Not all the titles known to the general public were taken into account, as in some cases they are less relevant to the overall context. However, many names described in the next pages are not as popular in the West, meaning that the book also tries to suggest new visions together with the mainstream ones.

As always happens in such a wide-ranging work, so many people have offered their precious suggestions to give a special insight into my book. I cannot mention everyone, but I especially thank Kusakabe Keiko, whose advice is always precious for my work; Giannalberto Bendazzi, who strongly believed in my project; Francesca Ellero for her empathy and careful and competent reading; directors Yamamura Kōji, Kuri Yōji, Sugii Gisaburō,

Shinkai Makoto, Yokosuka Reiko, Yusaki Fusako, Abe Yukio and Iimen Masako for direct and indirect aid.

Finally, for having shared most of my visions and infectious enthusiasm, I dedicate this book to my daughters Anja and Corinna.

Maria Roberta Novielli

About the Author

Maria Roberta Novielli has specialized in Japanese cinema at the Nihon University, Tokyo, Japan and now teaches history of cinema and animation in the Department of Philosophy and Cultural Heritage at the Ca' Foscari University of Venice, Venice, Italy. She is a contributor to numerous Italian and international magazines and books and author, among others, of *Storia del cinema giapponese* (*History of Japanese Cinema*, Marsilio, 2001), and *Animerama—Storia del cinema d'animazione giapponese* (*Animerama—History of Japanese Animated Cinema*, Marsilio, 2015). She is also the chief editor of Asian Media, the Italian website, which focuses on Asian cinema; the artistic director of the Venetian Ca' Foscari Short Film Festival; and the director of the master of fine arts in filmmaking at the Ca' Foscari University of Venice.

CHAPTER 1

From Pre-Cinema to the Birth of Industry

T HE FIRST ANIMATED MOVIE in Japan was presented in 1917, representing the most recent artistic development of the long-standing history of "moving images" in the country. Many important precursors had experimented with different kinds of visual storytelling, including the *emakimono* ("handscrolls") used from in the eleventh century by traveling storytellers to narrate legends and religious anecdotes.* The *emakimono* were held with both hands and slowly unrolled from the right to the left, so as to gradually let the images flow like a moving panorama, according to a chronological order of narration based on the poetry structure known as *kishōtenketsu*: *ki* ("enter") as an introduction, *shō* ("join and expand") as the development, *ten* ("turn") as the pivotal event and *ketsu* ("solution") as the ending.

Originated in the Chinese performative tradition, *kagee* ("shadow play") may be considered a precursor of animation in Japan.

---

* Among the oldest *emakimono*, also considered a precursor of Japanese comics, *Chōjū jinbutsu giga* ("Animal-Person Caricatures," shortened to *Chōjūgiga*) was attributed to the monk Toba Sōjō.

1

Very popular during the Edo period among both children and adults, practitioners often performed repertoires derived from the *kabuki* theater with musical background. Similarly, the magic lantern imported from the Netherlands at the end of the eighteenth century became very popular as an animation tool. Known as *utsushie* ("reflected pictures"), the original metal device was completely modified: made with wood and fitted with two lenses, it was easily portable and movable, and could accentuate the moving effect of the screened images. By the end of the nineteenth century, magic lanterns were also used in different contexts, such as in theaters, temples and schools, as a form of educational entertainment.

Among the street theater arts, which may be considered as precursors of animation, *kamishibai* ("paper play") has the longest history. Presumably dating back to the twelfth century, this form of storytelling reached its highest popularity during the 1920s and 1930s.* The itinerant presenters used to move from village to village, carrying a miniature stage-like device, in which different images could be alternated to narrate a story. During World War II, *kamishibai* was often used for propaganda purposes, not only due to its popularity but also because the storytellers could easily convey the nationalistic ideology.

The traditional *bunraku* puppet theater may be regarded as another source of inspiration; the theatrical form emerged in the seventeenth century when puppetry was coupled with the musical performances of *jōruri*. The puppets are animated by three performers known as *kuroko* ("black persons"), whose black clothes, including a hood, metaphorically hide their presence on the stage. Puppets have a complex system of joints, so that they can be easily moved, including their fingers and neck. However, their heads were not realistic and, classified by their gender and age, representing different human typologies: young women, warriors,

---

* During the 1950s, its popularity was gradually replaced by the spreading of TV sets, in the beginning called *denki kamishibai* ("electric *kamishibai*").

ghosts, demons and so on. Together with the figures of *ukiyoe* prints, these puppets are considered the ancestors of the stylized characters of most Japanese animations.

However, the media most similar to animation is undoubtedly *manga*, the Japanese comics, and its origin may be found in the cultural settings mentioned above, especially in *emakimono*. While woodblock prints and painting art were flourishing during the Edo period, the Japanese artist Hokusai created a collection of sketches known as *Hokusai Manga* (15 volumes published between 1814 and 1878), also presented at the Universal Exposition of Paris in 1867. This work, a collection of landscapes, animals and figures, is now considered the first *manga* in the modern sense of the word.

During the Meiji period, when Japan ended its isolation and opened its frontiers to other cultures, many newspapers and magazines introduced strips as part of their narration. The newborn cartoon magazine *Japan Punch*, which was published in Yokohama by English cartoonist Charles Wirgman, added some novelties. One example is putting text in balloons in the strips, which accounts for calling it *manga ponchi* (from the English word "punch") at the beginning of the twentieth century.

In 1905, the Japanese artist Kitazawa Rakuten (1876–1955, nom de plume Kitazawa Yasuji), strongly influenced by Western comics, established the satirical magazine *Tōkyō Puck*, where some of the pioneers of animation took their first steps. From 1912, artist Okamoto Ippei (1886–1948) became a renowned *manga kisha* ("comic journalist") for the *Asahi Newspaper*. His strips about chronicles and travel reports already contained many filmic elements, with new and dynamic effects. Decades later, "the God of manga" Tezuka Osamu asserted that he had been an admirer of both Kitazawa's and Okamoto's works.

PIONEERS

In July 2005, a fragment of an animated filmstrip (unknown author) was discovered in Kyoto. Fifty frames (about 4 seconds) of paintings on celluloid cels show a young man writing the word "cinema" (*katsudō shashin*, "images in movement," as it was called in that period) on a wall, who then turns toward the audience and greets the public, taking his hat off. According to Matsumoto Natsuki, the professor at Osaka University who had discovered the filmstrip along with some other animation historians, this movie was made in 1907,* which would make it the oldest animation in the world.

Until this filmstrip was found, historians had traced the first Japanese animation back to 1917, even if many foreign animated movies had already been screened in Japan before this date.† The pioneers of Japanese animation were Shimokawa Ōten, Kōuchi Jun'ichi and Kitayama Seitarō, all making their debut in 1917. Their works were unfortunately almost completely destroyed during the Great Kanto Earthquake of 1923. The growing popularity of foreign animation prompted the creation of departments inside the studios to experiment with the new art.‡ Among others, the Tennen Shoku Katsudō Shashin (Natural Color Moving Picture Company, known as Tenkatsu) in 1916 commissioned Shimokawa Ōten§ with making an animated short movie. He experimented with several techniques, including chalkboard animation, and in

---

* This theory has no real scientific basis, even if Japanese media launched the news on a big scale. It may presumably be a chromolitography for toy projectors, as the holes on the film seem to suggest.

† Some historians report that the first screening took place at the Asakusa Teikokukan in Tokyo on April 15, 1912. *Nippāru Transformations* (*Nippāru no henkei*, uncertain author), probably the Japanese title for *Les exploits de Feu-Follet* by Émile Cohl, was internationally distributed as *The Nipper's Transformations*. Other theories consider that *Le mobilier fidèle* (1910) by Cohl had been shown in Japan on September 1, 1911, and others consider that a series of animated movies, including Cohl's, had already been presented in 1910 with the overall title *New Picture Album of the Mischievous Boy* (*Dekobō shingachō*) (Litten, 2014).

‡ In the first period, animation was called *senga eiga* ("line pictures") and later *dōga eiga* ("animated films"). The word *anime* (a short for *animēshon*, "animation") was only used starting in the 1960s. Until the end of World War II, animated movies were also referred to as *manga eiga* ("manga cinema").

§ Nom de plume of Shimokawa Sadanori (1892–1973), an author of *mangas* known as Shimokawa Hekoten. He had been an assistant to Kitazawa Rakuten for the magazine *Tokyo Puck*.

the end, his first movie, a 5-minute short, was ready. *The Story of the Concierge Mukuzō Imukawa (Imokawa Mukuzō, genkanban no maki)* was distributed in January 1917 as the first Japanese animation. In the same year, Shimokawa made four other short movies, but because of his eye problems, he had to quit animation and worked only on comics, a field in which he became very famous.

The second pioneer, Kōuchi Jun'ichi (1886–1970, also known as Kōuchi Sumikazu), a former illustrator for the magazine *Tōkyō Puck*, was hired in 1916 by the production company Kobayashi Shōkai. His first short animated movie was *The Dull Sword (Hanawa Hekonai meitō no maki*, literally *Hanawa Hekonai's Sword*, also known with the title *Namakura katana)*, distributed on June 30, 1917. In this movie, a samurai complains to a merchant who sold him a dull sword, but the man scorns and even kicks him.* In his following works, Kōuichi also experimented with various techniques, such as using cels as frames for animation (invented in 1914 by Earl Hurd), shadow effects, synchronized sound,† and papercutting animation (*kirie*). In 1923, Kōuichi established his own production company, the Sumikazu Eiga, and specialized in folk stories; however, he soon abandoned animation to become a cartoonist, just like Shimokawa.

The third pioneer, Kitayama Seitarō (1888–1945), had previously been an illustrator for the *Contemporary Western Art (Gendai no yōga)* magazine and a collaborator of the post-impressionistic artistic group Fyūzankai. He joined the oldest Japanese production company, Nikkatsu (short for Nippon Katsudō Shashin Kabushiki Kaisha—Japan Motion Pictures Company, founded in 1912), and in 1915, he started working on his first animation, made with paintings on paper, *Battle of a Monkey and a Crab*

---

* For decades considered lost, an excerpt of the movie was rediscovered in an antique shop of Osaka in 2007.
† Obtained through the synchronization of records during the screenings. For both live and animated movies in Japan, the sound was usually performed by an orchestra and the stories read by a narrator (called *benshi* or *katsuben*).

(*Saru to kani no gassen*), presented only in 1917. The movie, now lost, was the adaptation of a traditional tale of the fourteenth century, but the style of the paintings was Western. Kitayama was the first artist to organize a staff of animators for his works, which allowed him to make more than 20 short movies in only 2 years. In 1921, he founded his own independent production company, the Kitayama Movie Laboratory (Kitayama Eiga Seisakujō), gathering some of the most talented illustrators, and soon specializing in commercials and educational short movies. The only work by Kitayama now visible is *Urashima Tarō* (ibid., 1918), digitalized in 2008 (the legendary history of a fisherman who follows a turtle under the sea), and an essay that he published in 1930, entitled *How to Make Animated Films* (*Sen eiga no tsukurikata*).[*]

These three pioneers paved the way for many young animators, some of whom had trained with them. In a few years, animation became a popular art and a field of uninterrupted experimentation.

CULTURAL TURMOIL

The Taishō Era (1912–1926) represented one of the liveliest periods in the history of Japan, invigorated by the urge for renewal and modernization and engaged in blending Western influences with the traditional culture of the country. Many media that had developed in the previous era—publishing industry, cinema and cartoons—quickly progressed, achieving their full maturity. During the 1920s, many cultural debates tried to define each media as a unique form of art, and animation would soon become an independent artistic expression.

Both live cinema and animation soon underwent governmental regulations. Among the others, in 1911, the Ministry of Education established the "Committee for the popular educational enquiry" (*Tsūzoku kyōiku chōsa iinkai*), in charge of

---

[*] Published in *Basic Facts for Film Education* (*Zen Nihon katsuei kyōiku kenkyūkai*), Tokyo, Japan, Kyōiku Shōkan, 1930, pp. 321–341.

controlling every entertainment field (including literature and cinema) (Salamon, 2002). In 1917, the committee formed a set of rules known as "Revision of the Provisions for the Regulation of Motion Pictures" (*Katsudō shashin kōgyō torishimari kisoku*), meant as a tool of moral tutelage. The committee also promoted the production of *kyōiku eiga* ("educational films"). Among the most influential, in 1917, Kitayama Seitarō made some shorts, such as *Recommendations for Your Savings* (*Chokin no susume*) and *Even Dust Piled Up Will Become a Mountain* (*Chiri mo tsumoreba yama to naru*), on behalf of the Ministry of Post and Telecommunication.

A prompt to the popularity of animation paroxysmally derived from the tragedy of the Great Kanto Earthquake of 1923, which almost completely destroyed the area of Tokyo and Yokohama, causing the deaths of over 100,000 people. In the aftermath of the destruction, the whole country worked hard to rebuild the architecture of the towns and to boost the morale of the survivors. Animation contributed to the recovery, presenting stories derived from tradition and mythology, able to give positive impulse to rise from the ashes stronger than before. For example, the young animator Yamamoto Sanae* made the optimistic *The Mountain Where the Old Women Are Abandoned* (*Ubasute yama*, 1923), based on an old legend according to which old people used to be taken to the top of a mountain to die, as they could not contribute to the community. However, in Yamamoto's movie, the protagonist of the story refuses to abandon his own mother, thus representing the possibility of overcoming the hardship of life.†

---

* Nom de plume of Yamamoto Zenjirō (1898–1981), who had trained with Kitayama Seitarō and later founded the independent Yamamoto Manga Productions. Many of his movies are adaptations from old legends, such as *Momotarō The Great* (*Nihon ichi Momotarō*, 1928), one of the most popular characters of Japanese folklore.

† The story was also adapted to the novel *The Ballad of Narayama* (*Narayama bushikō*, 1956), by Fukazawa Shichirō, and to two movies, both entitled *The Ballad of Narayama*, by Kinoshita Keisuke (1958) and Imamura Shōhei (1983).

Yamamoto also made some educational movies, including *Reforestation* (*Shokurin*, 1924) for the Ministry of Agriculture, *The Mail's Journey* (*Yūbin no tabi*, 1924) for the Ministry of Post and Telecommunication and *The Spread of Syphilis* (*Baidoku no denpa*, 1926) for the Ministry of Education.

ŌFUJI NOBURŌ

Thanks to his tireless experimentation and to the high quality of his work, in the 1960s the most prestigious award was established in his honor to recognize excellence and innovation in Japanese animation, a prize won by authors such as Miyazaki Hayao, Ōtomo Katsuhiro and Kon Satoshi. Ōfuji was also the first film director and animator to be internationally esteemed and receive awards in prestigious film festivals.

Ōfuji Noburō (Nom de plume of Ōfuji Shinshichirō, 1900–1961) started his career when he was only 18 years old as an apprentice to Kōuchi Jun'ichi. In 1921,* he founded his own production company, the Laboratory of Research on Free Cinema (*Jiyū Eiga Kenkyūjō* one year later renamed Chiyōgami Productions— *Chiyōgami Eigasha*), where he experimented with some new Western techniques, including mixing live action and animation (*A Story of Cigarettes—Kemurigusa monogatari*, 1924). Inspired by the silhouette animations by Lotte Reiniger, he made some works by using the Japanese *washi* paper painted in the *chiyōgami*[†] style. By advertising one of his first movies by using this technique, *Burglar of Baghdad Castle* (*Bagudajo no tōzoku*, 1926, inspired by *The Thief of Bagdad* by Raoul Walsh of 1924), novelty of style

---

* Uncertain year; 1921 is suggested in *Nihon eiga jinmei jiten* (*Dictionary of the Names of Japanese Cinema-Tokyo*, Japan, Kinema Junpōsha, 1997).
† This word means "paper" (*kami*) "of a thousand generations" (*chiyō*). It is painted with different patterns and colors and was used during the Edo period to make *chiyōgami ningyō* ("little dolls"), for origami and to upholster little boxes. Ōfuji used this paper, cutting figures and arranging them on backgrounds made with the same paper. Then by backlight, he obtained particular effects of shadowing and chromatic variations.

and comforting traditions were brought together: "the chiyōgami style offers a pure Japanese atmosphere" (Yamaguchi and Watanabe, 1977). Set in a traditional Japanese location, it is the story of a young man who falls in love with a princess and has to face many challenges to conquer her heart. All episodes are meant to convey moral precepts, as the recurring phrase "happiness may only be reached by bootstrapping yourself" suggests.

Ōfuji's works were not addressed to only children, but in many cases, they were expressly intended for adults. This is the case of *The Whale* (*Kujira*, 1927), which was also shown in Russia in the same year. Based on the Overture of Rossini's *William Tell*, this is the tale of three warriors and a woman who are swallowed by a whale after a shipwreck. Prompted by sexual desire, the men fight each other to possess the woman and to survive in the end, but the whale spits them out, the gods kill them and only the woman survives.

Music has always been an important component of Ōfuji's works. In 1931, he experimented with the improvement of record synchronization (Tōjō Eastphone technique) with the humoristic short movie *The Golden Flower* (*Kogane no hana*). He had already succeeded with synchronized sound (Eastphone Record) in a short movie of 1929, *The Black Cats* (*Kuronyago*), showing four children and two cats dancing on the notes of a traditional song for children. One could say that in Japan, music videos and karaoke started thanks to his animation, especially with the three short movies *Harvest Festival* (*Mura matsuri*, 1930), *Spring Song* (*Haru no uta*, 1931, a traditional melody performed by Inoue Kikuko), and *Kimigayo* (*Kokka Kimigayo*, 1931, the Japanese hymn). *Harvest Festival* shows the festival through a sequence of joyful events (mainly theatrical and dancing performances) and images, while at the bottom, the lyrics appear, showing the rhythm requested to sing, like the Fleischer brothers had already done in the United States. *Spring Song* (imbibed in pink) opens with a stave, on which notes and words gradually appear to introduce the music score. A sequence of scenes then shows anthropomorphic cherry flowers* and surreal figures dancing together on the basis of the musical rhythm. *Kimigayo* is made using black silhouettes on a gray background. It narrates the mythological origin of Japan, so as to highlight the "Japanese pure spirit" (*Yamato damashii*). The hymn words gradually appear on one side of the screen with no singing voice, so as to let the audience perform the vocal execution, a captivating collective experience for the period.†

ANIMATORS IN THE LIMELIGHT

In the 1910s and 1920s, a group of intellectuals launched the "Pure Film Movement" (*Jun eiga undō*), intended as a crossing point for suggestions aimed to make cinema independent of other arts, especially theater. To avoid the theatrical performative atmosphere, the narration in *benshis* had to be avoided and the cinematographic grammar enriched through a more complex expressive language. The Meiji period politics of cultural improvement‡ had already suggested referring to Western models to improve the quality of cinema, and animators also considered foreign works, especially the ones made in the United States, as a reference for their experimentation and a tool to acquire a personal and unique style to be possibly exported.

Stimulated by this changing atmosphere, many other innovative animators appeared in the same years of Ōfuji's intense experimentation, most of whom trained with the first pioneers and soon set about to trace their own personal paths. Among the most active ones, Murata Yasuji§ made his debut with

---

* The recurring cherry flowers and *hinomaru* (the Japanese flag) in this animation are a clear reference to the "Japanese spirit," in this period strongly emphasized; this is also the year when Japan invaded Manchuria.
† Both *Spring Song* and *Kimigayo* were also screened in the Taiwanese colony. For the distribution of Japanese movies in the colonies, also see Baskett (2008).
‡ Especially expressed by slogans such as "Eastern ethics and Western science" (*tōyō no dotoku, seiyō no gakugei*) and "Japanese spirit and Western techniques" (*wakon yōsai*).
§ Also known as Murata Yasushi (1896–1966), he began his training with Yamamoto Sanae and worked as a designer of captions for movies. As a filmmaker, he often worked with the director and illustrator Aoji Chūzō (1885–1970).

Why Is the Giraffe's Neck So Long? (*Jirafu no kubi wa naze nagai,* 1926). Starting from this first papercutting animation, it was evident that Murata's interest mainly concerned characters and locations originated from the Japanese tradition and folklore, such as zoomorphic beings, gods and magic atmospheres. The style of his works—regardless of the techniques he used—always revealed elegance, fluidity of movements, richness of details and an overall spectacularity. One needs to consider only the sophisticated *senga eiga* ("line-drawing film"), *The Stolen Lump* (*Kobutori,* 1929), as an example of his first movies based on an old Japanese tale. Two old neighbors, both with a lump on their faces, have very dissimilar personalities. Tarōhei is honest and a hard worker, while Jirōhei is lazy and a cheat. After falling asleep on the mountain where he was working, Tarōhei wakes up and sees a group of *tengus** dancing and playing music. He joins the dance and amuses them. The tengus magically remove his lump as compensation. When his neighbor tries to imitate him, his dance is inappropriate; in addition, he also tries to cheat the *tengus*, and for this, he is punished with the appearance of one more lump.

Using a mix of line-drawing animation, stop motion and live cinema, in that same year, Murata made *Tarō's Train* (*Tarō san no kisha*), which now represents one of the best examples of educational movies of the period. A boy gets a toy train from his father (this part is in live action); then, he falls asleep and the train animates and runs out of the box (in stop motion), thus becoming the setting of the boy's dream (in line-drawing animation). Inside the train, the boy is the conductor and all the passengers are animals. In a series of short animated sketches, this is a way to teach proper behavior on a train.

---

* A *tengu* is a fantastic creature considered both as a god and a supernatural monster. In this film, they are represented in two typologies: the "raven *tengu*" (*karasu tengu*) and the stronger "long-nose *tengu*" (*hanadaka tengu*).

Other interesting experiments by Murata followed in those years: *The Monkey Masamune* (*Saru Masamune*, 1930), where he used a papercut animation so fluid that it seems like a cel animation, enriched by a wide selection of angles and shots; in his first talkie, *The Unlucky Butterfly* (*Chō no sainan*, 1931), a huge selection of small movements offers the basis for amusing sound effects; finally, Murata used an extremely accurate narrative and graphic structure for his short movie *Sankō and the Octopus—A Fight Over a Fortune* (*Sankō to tako—Hyakuman ryō no chinsodo*, 1933), which also contains a scene where two octopuses kiss, an intimate aspect forbidden in live cinema till 1945.

Like Murata, Masaoka Kenzō (1898–1988, also known by his nom de plume Masaoka Donbei) was also a pioneer of different experiments. He was the first animator to use cels and the first to make a talkie with a real soundtrack. However, his first movie was a live action work, not an animation. In 1925, he was employed at Makino Productions, where he became one of Kinugasa Teinosuke's assistants. In 1927, he founded the independent Donbei Productions, which specialized in movies for children, but he had to quit after only 2 years. In 1929, he started a new job at the major studio Nikkatsu of Kyoto, where he was in charge of educational movies and began working on animation, making his debut with *Nonsense Story Vol. 1: Monkey Island* (*Nansensu monogatari daiippen—Sarugashima*, 1930). Finally, in 1932, Masaoka founded an independent studio, Masaoka Film Production (*Masaoka Eiga Seisakujō*), which specialized in animation. With the support of the major studio Shōchiku, in the same year, he made the first real talking animated movie in Japan, *The World of Power and Women* (*Chikara to onna no yo no naka*, 1932), supported by a staff of expert animators, including Kimura Hakusan and Seo Mitsuyo. The characters were dubbed by some of the most famous actors of the time, and the film had its premiere on April 15, 1933, at the Asakusa Teikokukan, on the same day and in the same place where the first Japanese animation had been presented in 1917.

In 1935, Masaoka joined the small JO (Jenkins-Ozawa) Production Company, where he made the spectacular *Princess Kaguya* (*Kaguyahime*, 1935) and earned the double epithet of being the "Japanese Méliès"—thanks to the huge variety of effects that he had included—and the "Japanese Disney" for his rich experimentation. He then founded a new independent company in 1937, the Masaoka Center for Film Research Masaoka Dōga Kenkyūjo.*

Kimura Hakusan (also Hakuzan, place and date of birth uncertain) had been Kitayama Seitarō's pupil and was also a collaborator of Masaoka at the Kitayama Eiga Seisakujō. After the Great Kanto Earthquake of 1923, he worked on *kyōiku eiga* ("educational movies") for the Asahi Kinema Gomeisha, the cinema department of the famous newspaper. He made his first movie in 1924, called *Akagaki Kenzō, A Sake Bottle Farewell* (*Akagaki Kenzō tokkuri no wakare*, 1924), but the oldest surviving movie is the educational *Frugal Tasuke Shiobara Saves Up* (*Kinken chochiku Shiobara Tasuke*, 1925), re-edited in 1941. This film, based on a kabuki play, presents the virtues of a self-made man, who works hard and honestly to elevate his own social position. After this work, Kimura received many commissions from the Ministry of Education, but in that same period, he was trying to find out his own artistic path. The result was a double record with the making of the first ever erotic and also censored animation movie, *Cool Ship* (*Suzumibune*, 1932).

Among the prestigious debut animators of these years, Ogino Shigeji (1899–1991) is considered the father of abstract animation in Japan. It has been calculated that his work counts about 400 titles made up to the 1970s, some of which were awarded international prizes. Among the others, in 1935, he won first prize at the International Film Contest of Budapest for three movies—all made in the same year—*Rhythm* (id.), *Expression* (*Hyōgen*) and *Propagate* (*Kaika*). Ogino had started making movies at the end of the 1920s by using a Pathé Baby, but in the following years, he also used different formats—8, 9.5 and 16 mm experimenting

---

* It was the first time the word *dōga* was used as a synonym for animation.

with various styles and techniques, including film coloring and kodachrome shooting, not only in animation but also in travel documentaries. His experimental movies afforded him a means to explore the potential of cinema and to give form to his fervid imagination due to which he has often been compared to Oskar Fischinger. Lines and forms alternate on the screen in a chromatic and abstract choreography, producing dreamlike sequences of symbols as in *Rhythmic Triangles–Fight Among Cards (Sankaku no rizumu—Toranpo no arasoi*, 1932).

ON GODS, MONSTERS AND STRANGE CREATURES

The first American animations had already been shown in Japan in the 1920s, but their distribution only became systematic starting in the early 1930s, especially thanks to the Tokyo office of Paramount. They were mainly talkies, especially Fleischers' *Talkertoons* and Disney's *Silly Symphonies*. Some of their characters soon became extremely popular, such as Betty Boop,* Mickey Mouse, Felix the Cat and Popeye, but at the same time, the growing nationalistic ideology was identified; for example, Mickey Mouse represented American culture, and before long, the popularity of such characters decreased.

The greatest influence exerted by American artists on Japanese animators probably consisted of the protoplasmic approach to human representation, metamorphosed into animal traits of various typologies. The anthropomorphic beasts could also represent a light alternative to everyday life in a period of hardship, like economic depression,† because animals could perform excessive and

---

* The episode *Ha! Ha! Ha!* (1934) was even quoted in one of the most popular Japanese live action movies in the same year, *Our Neighbour, Miss Yae (Tonari no Yaechan)* by Shimazu Yasujirō. To increase her popularity, in 1935, the short *A Language All My Own* was presented—somehow an homage to Japan, where Betty Boop flies to Tokyo and even sings in Japanese, wearing a kimono.

† A fundamental analysis of animal iconography in animation, especially referring to the *Silly Symphonies* series, was made in 1941 by Sergei Eisenstein. His theories, together with other evaluations on the totemic nature of animals, are widely described in Wells (2009).

grotesque situations with comic effects. They are, for instance, immune to death and can adapt to any living form (Mickey Mouse and Pluto, representing a man and an animal, respectively). In the Japanese context especially, they can also be compared to gods, given their polysemous characteristics in relation to the local mythology.

Some ancient god-animals are still very popular in animation, and in the 1930s, they populated the Japanese scene. For instance, *inari*, gods related to rice, could easily turn into astute and vengeful foxes (*kitsune*), which can also transform into human beings, especially women who tempt men and sometimes even suck their blood. Cats (*neko*) may have a positive and a negative meaning. They can transform into human beings (called *bakeneko*) and, in their worst form, they are often selfish and insensible. Spiders are sneaky demons, able to trap their victims into their web, and often represented with big, round eyes and sharp teeth. According to Buddhism, butterflies are positive because they symbolize the Japanese spirit, since they pass through different conditions before achieving their final state of beauty (that is, nirvana). Carp have a positive connotation, being the symbol of youth, courage, strength and perseverance.

These are only some examples of the most common animals recurring in animation. One should also consider the wide pantheon of mythological figures that share only some characteristics with animals. *Tengus* and *tanukis* are among the most popular ones. *Tengus* are shintoist amoral spirits who live in mountain forests. They harass those who do not respect them and reward those who gratify them. They represent a symbol of freedom, since they are proud and independent and acknowledge only their head as the authority.

An example of *tengu* has already been discussed above in relation to the movie *The Stolen Lump* by Murata Yasuji; the films in which they make their appearance are numerous in this period. Ōfuji Noburō's cel animation *The Routing of the Tengu* (*Tengu taiji*, 1934, made under the nom de plume Koyamano Furō) is one of the best remaining examples. Distributed in both a sound and a silent version, it is also considered a kind of response to the popularity of Betty Boop, since the facial features of the characters resemble hers, and the duel scenes—two *tengus* that kidnap a geisha and fight with a samurai—are choreographically described with a rhythm similar to her dances.

Like *tengus*, *tanukis*ˊ were also extremely popular. They have always been considered to be mythological figures with extraordinary powers. They are cheerful, lovable, cute and benevolent shape-shifting creatures with a passion for *sake* and the habit of drumming their own bellies. They show an open rivalry with foxes. Many popular animations were dedicated to them. Among the others, *The Teapot Bunpuku* (*Bunpuku chagama*, 1928, by Murata Yasuji) tells of a *tanuki*, which transforms into a teapot to be sold to a temple, so as to reward the man who had rescued it; once back in its original form, the animal throws the temple into disarray. In 1934, Masaoka Kenzō made *Dance of the Teakettles* (*Chagama ondo*, the first Japanese animation completely in cels), where some *tanukis* are lured into a temple by the sound of a gramophone and try to steal it. One of the best titles dedicated to these animals is *Moving Pictures—Fox Vs. Racoon Dogs* (*Ugokie Kori no tatehiki*, 1933) by Ōishi Ikuo (also known as Ōishi Iku, 1901–1944), in which two *tanukis* and a fox—clearly resembling Felix the Cat—have a terrible fight, and a series of magic effects and metamorphoses turn them into *yōkai* ("supernatural monsters").

THE DIVERSIFICATION IN GENRES

During the 1920s, the live cinema industry in Japan had already diversified its productions into various genres, often adapting novels belonging to the so-called popular literature (*taishū bungaku*) to the screen. Many of the stories, set in the past and called period drama (*jidaigeki*), especially in the great duels (*daikettō*)

ˊ *Inyctereutes procyonoides* or "raccoon dog" is a canid indigenous of East Asia, similar to raccoons and badgers.

scenes, had refined the action dynamics according to a style called *chanbara.* The influence of the spectacular contemporary American action cinema well matched the Japanese epics of warriors and stoicism in battle.

The animation industry soon began the production of the same kind of movies, where *chanbara* often represented the main dramatic scenes. Some of the movies mentioned in the previous pages belong to this genre, and many others were produced in the 1930s. One of the most interesting ones is again signed by Murata Yasuji, *The Bat* (*Kōmori*, 1930), which displays many choral scenes—including many comic shots—in which birds fight against terrestrial animals, while a bat alternately and opportunistically sides with one of the two factions, thanks to its double nature of being a flying mammalian.

The *chanbara* action atmosphere was also well matched with the growing militaristic spirit of the era, which explains the growing number of short movies on battles and heroes at the time. The same spirit of self-denial and sacrifice given to the main characters, which are particularly loved by the younger audience, can be found in the contemporary movies dedicated to sports,† where the pathos consists of the tension given by the *Agon* of competition and self-edification. Starting from the Olympic Games of Amsterdam in 1928, many sport movies were produced, including *The Animal Olympics* (*Dōbutsu Orinpikku taikai*, 1928) by Murata Yasuji and Aoji Chūzō and *Olympic Games on Dankichi Island* (*Dankichijima no Orinpikku taikai*, 1932, unknown author). Elephants, geese, pigs, and many other animals compete, causing very funny and surreal situations. Different sports were represented, including the native *sumo* (for example, *Animal Sumo*—*Dōbutsu sumo taikai*, 1931, unknown author), and the exotic baseball (like in *Our Baseball Match*—*Oira no yakyū*, 1931, by Aoji Chūzō with drawings by Murata), a way to give an indigenous touch to this sport imported from the United States

---

* The genre *kengeki* (*ken* means "sword") was popularly known as *chanbara*, an onomatopoeic word—*chan chan bara bara*—derived from the clatter of swords during the duels.

† Among the first animation on sport in Japan, in 1923, Yamamoto Sanae made *The Hare and the Tortoise* (*Usagi to kame*, adapted from the famous Aesop tale).

a few decades before. During the following Olympic Games held in Los Angeles in 1932, Japanese athletes won many medals, an event that increased the popularity of these movies. Think of the success of *Sports Day at Animal Village* (*Dōbutsu mura no supotsu dē*, 1932) by Murata and Aoji. Moreover, many of these works were also meant as specific educational movies, such as *A Day of Chameko* (*Chameko no hi*), an interesting animation—a hybrid between sport movies and musicals—made by Nishikura Kiyoji in 1931. The story is set in 1929 and shows a well-behaved young girl during an ordinary day of her life, from the moment she wakes up to her sport activities, including a live cameo by the Olympic-winning Japanese athlete Kinue Hitomi.

Also, musicals became very popular in this period, as many of Ōfuji's works mentioned in the previous pages demonstrate. Among the most successful and well-made animations, one should mention *Home Alone Mice* (*Nezumi no rusuban*, 1931, by Ōishi Ikuo), where some mice dance and dream about defeating a big cat. This movie is interesting because the features of the mice are quite similar to the contemporary Mickey Mouse but with some Japanese peculiarities, such as the *hachimaki*, the traditional headband symbol of perseverance and courage, which they wear when they fight against the cat.

Among the film genres of this period, science fiction makes its debut with some short animations such as, *The Plane Cabby's Lucky Day* (*Ooatari sora no entaku*, 1932) by Katō Teizō. The story takes place in 1980; animals populate the ground, and human beings live on top of skyscrapers. The main character is a "plane taxi driver;" he helps an injured eagle and is thus rewarded by the bird who shows him how to find a treasure, with which he will be able to look after his elderly mother. Many virtues promoted by the militaristic credo are contained in this story: not only the need for cooperation* but also the importance of the familiar cohesion, where "family" may be a synonym for empire.

---

* In fact, the final phrase is included at the end of the movie as a title: "Compassion is a good investment."

CHAPTER 2

Winds of War and Reconstruction

E MPEROR HIROHITO ASCENDED TO the throne, heralding the Shōwa era in 1926, even if he had been de facto Prince Regent (*Sesshō*) from 1921, when his father Yoshihito was deemed mentally and physically incompetent to reign. It was evident that his politics would promote a strong nationalistic credo when his government increased the supervision of media: from 1925 to 1931—the year of the invasion of Manchuria—the Police Affairs Bureau of the Home Ministry gradually tightened up the regulations on cinema with the aim to partially restrict creative freedom, so as to preserve the national spirit.

Meanwhile, the social turmoil of the period caused by the economic crisis had facilitated the diffusion of the Marxist ideologies and the birth of cultural associations such as the leftist All Japan Council of Proletarian Art Groups (*Zen Nihon musansha geijutsu dantai*, shortened to NAPF, founded in 1928), which soon became one of the main victims of the new regulations.* *Prokino* (Proletarian Cinema) was founded on February 2, 1929 by the two film critics Iwasaki Akira† and Sasa Genjū. It spread in different parts of the country and became the means for Japanese groups of intellectuals to present the instances of their ideology‡—resulting in increasing diffusion of amateur production in 9, 5 and 16 mm after the popularity of Pathé Baby and Eastman Kodascope in the 1920s.

In 1926, a small group of young animators founded the Baby Cinema Club (*Bebī Kinema Kurabu*) in the Kansai area (including Osaka, Kobe and Kyoto), as well as a smaller association in Kyoto called the Association of Baby Cinema of Kyoto (*Kyōto Bebī Shinema Kyōkai*), whose members had strict connections with Prokino (Makino, 2006). In 1929, the leader Nakano Takao and the student Tanaka Yoshitsugu established the Dōeisha company, where Tanaka and other young filmmakers made their amateur shorts in 16 mm by using the silhouette technique. In 1929, after *The Story of Alibaba* (*Aribaba monogatari*, 1929) and *Little Thumb* (*Issunboshi*, 1929), he made *The Chimney Sweeper* (*Entotsuya Perō*, 1930), an anti-war manifesto that had somehow never been censored. One day in a town called Tam Tom, the chimney sweeper Perot saves a bird threatened by an

---

* Especially starting from 1931, censors accentuated their control on NAPF. After the murder of Prime Minister Inukai Tsuyoshi in 1932 by a group of ultra-nationalist Navy officers—an event that triggered the total militarist politics of the country—the regulations became even stricter. The definitive turning point occurred in 1933 with the so-called "season of apostasy" (*tenkō no kisetsu*), when many leftist intellectuals were compelled to publicly denounce Marxists as thought criminals. Among the victims of the persecution was animator Seo Mitsuyo (1911–2010, nom de plume of Norikazu Seo, in some cases Seo Tarō), who had also been jailed for 3 weeks, before becoming the author of some of the most important propaganda animations.

† Iwasaki was also the author of the animation *The Three Little Bears* (*Sanbiki no koguma san*, 1931), based on a short novel by Murayama Kazuko, wife of the leftist avant-garde artist Murayama Tomoyoshi.

‡ Their movies, which included political films, documentaries and animations, used to be screened in small halls, and their theories published in the magazine *Proletarian Cinema* (*Puroretaria Eiga*). The movement lasted only three years.

eagle, and as a reward, he receives a magic egg that can "produce" soldiers. Later, he accidentally destroys the prince's personal train and is condemned to death, but when enemy forces arrive in the city, he saves his country thanks to the magic egg, ignoring that the war had already begun. When he realizes how hideous war is, he gives the egg up with a last desire: "Let the wars disappear!"

After *Prokino* productions had been censored, in 1933, Tanaka Yoshitsugu, Nakano Takao and other young filmmakers of Dōeisha entered the animation department of JO Studios,* where they made many other experimental movies, sometimes in cooperation with different production companies.† Ichikawa Kon, one of the most famous Japanese live cinema directors, author of masterpieces like *The Burmese Harp* (*Biruma no tategoto*, 1956) and *Fires on the Plain* (*Nobi*, 1959) made his debut at JO Studios as an animator. An enthusiast of Disney's animations, when he was only 18 years old he wrote the script, directed, animated and edited the cel animation for *The New Story of the Crackle Mountain* (*Shinsetsu kachikachi yama*, 1936), a sequel to the fairy tale of a trouble-making *tanuki* and a hare.‡

In 1936, a building contractor in Tokyo, Kobayashi Ichizō, who was also the president of the railroad line Minoo Arima, invested a large amount of money in show business to put a sheen to the line. He built and acquired many cinemas and then founded the all-female theater group *Takarazuka Kagekidan* (Opera Takarazuka). He also acquired the PCL (Photo Chemical Laboratories, which

---

* The J, which precedes Osawa's initial letter, refers to the Jenkins sound system, for which he had acquired the rights. The company was later renamed Talkie JO Studios (JO Tōkī Sutajo).
† Among others, with the major studio Shōchiku they cooperated in making the first talkie by Masaoka Kenzō, and, with the same filmmaker, the experimental *Air Strike Against Air Defenses* (*Kūshū tai bōkū*, 1934), with the set completely built in miniature (Hagihara, 2009).
‡ Ichikawa also made a second animation a few years later, *The Girl at the Dojō Temple* (*Musume Dojōji*, 1945).

specialized in sound recording) and JO Studios, merging them with the major studio Tōhō, which would soon become one of the greatest animation producers of Japan.

NATIONALISM NEEDS HEROES

The nationalistic creed underwent many hikes, especially in connection with the main militaristic landmarks of the period. In 1931, the date of the invasion of Manchuria; on February 26, 1936, when a group of young imperial army officers attempted a coup d'état assassinating several government members; in 1937, with the beginning of the Sino-Japanese war; and in 1941, with the attack on Pearl Harbor and the declaration of war on the United States and the British Empire. As a result, animation authors made an increasing number of movies where the main characters, especially those derived from mythology, better represented the perfect Japanese people, both in past and contemporary settings.

One of the most important icons that appeared in the Taishō era was Norakuro, a contraction for stray dog (*nora inu*) and Kurokichi (the name of the character). First presented in a series of mangas by Tagawa Suihō published from 1931 to 1941 in the magazine *The Youth's Club* (*Shōnen Kurabu*) by the editor Kōdansha,* the description of this character slightly changed over the years according to social and politics nuances. In the beginning, Norakuro enrolled in the regiment of *mōken rentai* ("brave dogs") as a second-class private, but it barely adapted to the strict military discipline, causing a series of funny situations. Gradually, it became capable of fighting against other animals, slowly rising through the ranks.

With its characterization similar to Felix the Cat and due to the surreal situations in its everyday life, it was easy for common people to identify with Norakuro, which in time lost its clumsiness. Among the animated versions of the manga, Norakuro appears

---

* The founder and president of Kōdansha, Noma Seiji, was a fervent nationalist.

as lazy and bungling in *Private Second-class Norakuro* (*Norakuro nitōhei*, 1933, by Murata Yasuj), then as brave and resolute—even if only in a dream—in *Corporal Norakuro* (*Norakuro gochō*, 1934, by Murata), and in the end as a real hero against a group of spies in *Second Lieutenant Norakuro: Sunday Magic* (*Norakuro Shōi: Nichiyōbi no kaijiken*, unknown author and year).

Through Norakuro's adventures, the audience could learn many details about the war, such as how to use weapons, the way battalions were organized and the spirit of self-sacrifice and pride for the country. In Japanese live cinema, the enemy was never shown, preferring to emphasize the courage of the soldiers; while in animation, the antagonists were simply represented as animals of a different species—that is, the dog Norakuro against monkeys or pigs. According to Thomas Lamarre, "Norakuro films depict friend and foe as humanoid animals, or precisely, as animalized humans. Animals on both sides appear cute, playful, childlike, elastic and plastic. Instead of humanism then, this sort of animation develops an 'animalism' mingled with animism, vitalism and what might be called 'childism'" (Lamarre, 2008). This approach thus helps to meld races, representing war as a chance at freedom for a wider population, the kind that was supposed to derive from the pan-Asiatic expansion.

Halfway between mythology and legend, Momotarō* is one of the protagonists of this period, a character with a strong forging power, like Mickey Mouse in the United States. The original legend tells of an old couple who finds a peach from which a prodigious child is born. When the boy is fifteen years old, he leaves for the near Onigashima (Island of *oni*, the demons), where some girls have been imprisoned; he is followed by a dog, a pheasant and a monkey that he meets during his travel. After defeating the *onis*, Momotarō goes back home, bringing treasure with him. Murata Yasuji, in cooperation with Aoji Chūzō, dedicated two short

---

* We already met an animated example in the previous chapter with the movie *Momotarō The Great* (1928) by Yamamoto Sanae.

movies to this hero in the beginning of the 1930s: *Momotarō's Sky Adventures* (*Sora no Momotarō*, 1931) and *Momotarō's Underwater Adventures* (*Umi no Momotarō*, 1932)—both showing the young hero in battles against an eagle (in the first movie) and a shark (in the second one), to save innocent animals. These movies are full of details about war strategies: for example, through the accurate description of the charts and the gas stations, the dynamics of air raids, the mechanics of airplanes and submarines, and so on.

Momotarō is also one of the leading characters of *Toy Box Series—Episode 3 Black Cat Banzai* (*Omochabako shirīsu—Daisanwa Kuroneko Banzai*, 1934, by Nakano and Tanaka). The black cat (Kuroneko, featured like Felix the Cat) happily lives with some dolls and other toys on an island. One day, an evil "Mickey Mouse" (riding a bat with his same features and followed by a similar fleet) attacks the island, threatening the inhabitants with a terrestrial battalion of snakes and a maritime fleet of crocodiles. Many legendary heroes appear from a magic book entitled *Old Japanese Fairy Tales—Momotarō* (*Nihon mukashi banashi Momotarō*), starting from the brave Momotarō, who soon defeats the invaders. The choice of representing the defeated mouse as a limping and old character is indeed interesting—a symbol for the decline of the West, while many cherry flowers blossom together as an icon of the young Japanese empire.

Like the young David who beats Goliath, another famous hero is Issunbōshi (*issun* is a unit of measurement of about 3 centimeters; *bōshi* means "son"), the Japanese Tom Thumb, born as a gift from the gods to an old couple longing for a child. When he is fifteen years old, Issunbōshi leaves for Kyoto in search of a job, taking a needle that he will use as a sword and a bowl and chopsticks as a boat. Employed by a noble family, one day he goes to a temple with their young daughter, who is assaulted by two demons. Thanks to his small size, Issunbōshi manages to jump into the demons' throats, cutting them from the inside and killing them. Wearing the demons' magic cape, he transforms into a taller and normal man and marries the young girl.

Some of the first animated adaptations of this tale are faithful to the original story, such as *The Tiny One Makes It Big* (*Issunbōshi no shusse*, 1929, unknown author). However, in some animations of this period, the war atmosphere becomes clear. In *Tiny Chibisuke's Big Adventure** (*Issunbōshi: Chibisuke monogatari*, 1935, by Seo Mitsuyo), not only some war tools are displayed. The demon peeks at the princess by using a submarine telescope and some match boxes simulate tanks, to fight the antagonist, the little hero also replicates himself by means of a magic stamp, producing an army of identical figures, which becomes an important metaphor for the power acquired by belonging to a group. In the end, all the clones blend into a normal-size man who marries the young girl, as in the original tale.

The legendary Urashima Tarō, also very popular in this period, can be considered a kind of anti-hero. While fishing alone, he rescues a turtle. As a reward, the animal invites the man to the Dragon Palace (called *Ryūgū*) under the sea. There, the turtle transforms into a beautiful woman, one of the king's daughters, and they marry, living happily together. After three days, Urashima feels nostalgic for his home and family. Before he leaves, the princess gives him a magic box, which will allow him to return to her whenever he wants, provided that he never opens it. Back home, the man realizes he has been away for 300 years and none of his family or friends are still alive. Upset, he opens the box and suddenly gets old and dies, turning to dust.

Animators have dedicated many works to this character. One of the first adaptations was made in 1918 by Kitayama Seitarō. A copy of this movie was rediscovered together with *The Dull Sword*, later restored and imbibed in pink. In 1925, Kimura Hakusan gave an original interpretation of the tale with *The Easy-going Old Man Visits the Ryūgū* (*Nonkina tōsan Ryūgū mairi*, also known as *The Dream of Urashima—Yume no Urashima*†). Urashima is a lazy

---

* The word *Chibisuke*, like Issunbōshi, means "little man".
† The film adapted the bestselling manga *Easygoing Daddy* (*Nonkina tōsan*) by Asō Yutaka.

man who dreams that he has been to the Dragon Castle, but, on returning to his family, no one recognizes him any longer. When he wakes up, he finally understands the value of working and of having a family. Some classical versions followed, like the ones by Ōfuji Noburō in 1928 and by Miyashita Manzō in 1931, both simply entitled *Urashima Tarō*. The cornerstone of all these movies is the magical element and the passing of time, as well as the basic negativity of the leading character: not only does he avoid the responsibilities toward his family and work and escapes to a different world, but he is also unable to keep his promise not to open the box, suffering the consequences. The popularity of this anti-hero can also be ascribed to the ancient love and fear of Japanese people for the sea and its creatures, considered an arcane place, where one can disappear, and, at the same time, a source of life, thanks to fishing.

IN THE MOOD FOR HORROR

Many horror films, both live action and animation, were produced during the 1930s. It is especially in the more severe periods of economic depression or war that this genre gains a wider popularity, since it better interprets the people's common sense of anxiety and social fragility. Moreover, Japanese mythology enumerates many semi-human creatures populating everyday contexts, often exorcised through specific rituals, such as fireworks, festivals and mystic functions. For centuries, these figures have been protagonists of the horror repertoire in art, especially from the Edo period (1603–1868), as the famous *ukiyoe* woodblock prints by Tsukioka Yoshitoshi, Utagawa Hiroshige and Katsushika Hokusai demonstrate. Literature and theater also include many horror stories and plays of the past, especially those related to the *kaidan* (tales of phantoms of Chinese origin). In these short novels, where the oneiric sense of the plots becomes a metaphor for human chaos and the physical transformations act as a symbol of impermanence.

Creatures such as *tengus* and *tanukis*, phantoms (*yūrei**) and supernatural entities (*yōkai*) can barely be categorized according to the dualism of a Manichean view. They live on the Earth, not in the Underworld, and they are often iconographic representations of some human aberrations—which also explains their anthropomorphic aspect.† Independent and unbound to any social order, they are amoral rather than evil: their good or bad behavior depends on the human being who approaches them, like many funny animations of the 1930s demonstrate. Among others, *Ban Danaemon's Monster Hunt at Shōjō Temple* (*Shōjōji no tanuki bayashi Ban Danaemon*, 1935, by Kataoka Yoshitarō‡) represents a good example of the classic imagery on phantoms, even if blended with some Western elements. Particularly interesting is the portrayal of the leading character, the legendary samurai Ban Danaemon of the Edo period, known for his courage and extraordinary force, a figure that would ideally fit the nationalistic credo of the era. In this film, he is an anti-hero, who accepts the task of freeing a castle haunted by *tanukis* to get a monetary reward to buy alcoholic drinks. At the end, the samurai and the lord of the castle celebrate the defeat of the invaders, having *tanuki* soup for dinner, an element that suggests how human beings can be crueler than monsters.

Other similar animations fit the period exalting their heroes: *Hatanosuke and the Haunted House* (*Hinomaru Hatanosuke: Bakemono yashiki no maki*, unknown author, presumably made in 1935), based on the nationalistic mangas by Nakajima Kikuo, presents the samurai as an invincible and dignified warrior.

---

* Classic phantoms are spirits coming back among living people for revenge, in this sense specifically called *onryō* or *goryō*. Their negativity thus results from the injustice they suffered when alive.

† They are also related to the Shinto eight million gods (*yaoyorozu no kami*), who symbolize different human values and ideals.

‡ A longer version of the same movie was presented with sound in 1939. The title refers to a song for children, which is also used in another animation of the period, *Story of Tanukis at the Shōjō Temple* (*Shōjōji no tanukibayashi*, 1935, by Ōishi Ikuo).

Similarly, the young protagonist of *Taro's Monster Hunt* (*Furudera no obake sodo*, 1936, by Suzuki Hiromasa˙) is able to overcome his fear and defeat the demons, mocking them in the end. A very particular horror animation is *A Night at the Bar* (*Izakaya no hitoya*, 1936, by Murata Yasuji). The young protagonist is unemployed, but even though he is broke, he orders some drinks in a bar and falls asleep. He dreams of himself waking on the bottom of the sea, where he meets two samurais. The young man persuades them to follow him into a Western phantom ship, where a treasure is supposed to be hidden, but there, the samurais have to fight against a crew of Western skeletons (more realistic and thus more frightening than the Japanese phantoms), while the young man runs away, stealing the treasure. Even if it is only in the timespan of a dream, the boy becomes a true anti-hero, who is both a coward and cunning. However, the audience is attracted to him because being unemployed makes him one of them. In this sense, this may be considered as one of the rare examples of anti-propaganda films of the period.

PROPAGANDA CINEMA—*KOKUSAKU EIGA*

Cinema and animation should exalt the traditional Japanese culture of the past, so as to ideally represent the war efforts that the country would be expected to endorse: this is only one of the principles strengthened by the regulations related to cinema during the 1930s. Indoctrination through media was widespread and effective, able to elevate any individual participation to the level of the collective ideal.

In April 1939, the new law on cinema (*Eigahō*) was introduced, and the following year, it was integrated with new regulations. Based on the model of the Nazi *Spitzenorganisation der Filmwirtschaft*, it was made of twenty-six articles aimed to elevate *kokumin bunka no kōjō* ("national culture"). According to the new law, a census of all people working in cinema had to be taken and

---

˙ Also known as Ashida Iwao.

the scripts of the movies checked, so as to avoid destabilizing topics: mainly criticism toward the government, the usage of foreign words, female characters behaving like Western women (for example, smoking and drinking in bars), and so on. Alternatively, the law solicited the introduction of subject matter such as the divine power of the Emperor, the importance of family, the spirit of self-sacrifice and the need for a collective effort in farming, industry and war activities. In brief, on one hand, this law repressed any form of individualism and freedom, while on the other hand, it indicated the only contents that could be admitted in films, therefore launching the birth of a new film genre: movies for lifting *sen'i kōyō eiga* (the "fighting spirit").

Considered as a monad of the Empire, many animations proposed models of the ideal family, where all members cooperate to live happily—a way to incentivize demographic increase. One of the best examples is in *The Animal Village in Trouble* (*Dōbutsu mura no daisodo*, uncertain year by Yamamoto Sanae) where three neighboring families (the *Tanukis*, the Bears and the Monkeys) live in a small village. While the *Tanukis* and the Bears live calmly because they have only one child each, the Monkey parents are quite busy with their numerous children. However, during a storm, the Monkeys join their forces and succeed in saving both themselves and their neighbors, demonstrating how a large family is safer than the smaller ones.

Like live-action cinema, animation also gave great importance to children in a genre called *shōnen mono* ("youth cinema"), exalting the innocence, and of their sense of moral duty, which is easily malleable. Some of the most popular animated characters derived from manga were symbols of successful young boys, such as Mābo in *Mābo's Big Race* (*Mābo no daikyoso*, 1936, unknown author), who competes in various sports at the Olympic games[*] against Western athletes.

---

[*] His adversaries are supported by a very peculiar audience, including some icons such as Betty Boop and Mickey Mouse.

Mābo is also the leading character of a historical movie (*rekishi eiga*), dated 1938, *Mābo as Kinoshita Tokichirō* (*Mābo no Kinoshita Tokichirō*, 1938, unknown author), acting as a *rōnin* (a masterless samurai) who seeks a lord to be at the service of. This movie is peculiar because it shows the metamorphosis of samurais into war machines (for example, their armor, which transforms into tanks), and also because of the uncommon ending, which reveals a camera and a filmmaker, thus suggesting that everything is fictional.

Some magniloquent historical figures recurred to praise the grandeur of the past, as in the adaptation of the twelfth century General Minamoto Yoshitsune in the protagonist Ushiwaka of an animation by Masaoka Kenzō, entitled *Benkei Vs. Ushiwaka* (*Benkei tai Ushiwaka*, 1939). Fundamental are the scenes dedicated to the instruction of Ushiwaka in the art of the sword, trained by a powerful *tengu*. Among the other works dedicated to the training of heroes, *Tarō's Early Training Days* (*Hinomaru Tarō: Musha shugyō no maki*, 1936, by Suzuki Atsushi) even opens with the statement "I am Tarō, hero of the poor and the weak" before beginning the long training.*

When referring to armies instead of single heroes, the characters were often animals of different species, as in the case of monkeys in *The Monkey Fleet* (*Osaru no kantai*, 1936, by Miyashita Manzō), where they fight against a battalion of octopuses. Very popular were the animations dedicated to the monkeys of the Sankichi Unit. In *Sankichi The Monkey: The Storm Troopers* (*Osaru no Sankichi: Totsugekitai*, 1934, by Seo Mitsuyo), a battle among them and polar bears also refers to the three human bullets (*nikudan san'yūshi*)—three soldiers based in Shanghai who on February 22, 1932, launched themselves against a Chinese fortification, carrying a twelve-foot-long bamboo pole stuffed with explosives. Repeatedly reported by media, this episode also became the subject of stage and radio plays and

---

* In live-action cinema, one of the best examples of the training of a hero is represented by *Sugata Sanshirō* (1943) by Kurosawa Akira.

even of popular songs, glorified as a symbol of self-sacrifice and cohesion among soldiers.

Most propaganda movies were set in the air or on the sea (sometimes on some islands), the two natural borders of Japan that needed to be protected.* In some cases, this was clearly stressed, for example, in *Sankichi The Monkey: The Air Combat* (*Osaru no Sankichi: Bokusen*, 1942, by Kataoka Yoshitarō), which opens with the title "Let's protect our sky" and emphatically ends with the statement "There will always be other enemies, we must protect our sky." Outside the country, the main sets are the Empire's colonies, a means to demonstrate how the Japanese were actually educating the noble savages. As an example, in *Dankichi on a Tropical Island* (*Bōken Dankichi - Hyoryū no maki*, author and year unknown),† a young boy teaches savages how to battle and becomes their king. Some movies show the advantages expected from colonization: in *Tarō Overseas* (*Kaikoku Tarō: Shin Nihonjima banzai*, 1938, by Suzuki Hiromasa), the protagonist saves the inhabitants of an island from a lion attack and discovers a gold mine; the shortage of minery sources in Japan was one of the reasons that led to the pan-Asiatic expansion.

The most lyrical movie dedicated to the colonies is likely *The Spider and the Tulip* (*Kumo to churippu*, 1943, by Masaoka Kenzō), a short animation of 16 minutes made with 20,000 cels synchronized with a pre-recorded soundtrack.‡ It tells of a spider that tries to trap a tender ladybug into its web, but the insect protects itself inside a tulip. In the end, the spider is blown away by a violent storm. The propaganda elements are mainly represented by the features of the three protagonists: the spider, the ladybird, and the tulip. The spider

---

* In other movies, enemies have sneaked into the country as spies, such as the ones sent by Roosevelt and Churchill to Japan in *Defeat of the Spies* (*Supai gekimetsu*, 1942, by Yamamoto Sanae).

† Dankichi is the leading character of a popular manga by Shimada Keizō, published from 1933 to 1939 in Kōdansha's magazine *Shōnen kurabu*.

‡ Music has a paramount function in this film: the ladybird sings a song for children (with the voice of Sugiyama Yoshiko), while the baritone Murao Gorō's powerful voice performs the mellow song of the spider.

is sketched according to the stereotypes of Afro-Americans (black, with full lips, smoking a pipe); the childish and innocent ladybird represents Asian colonies; and they are protected by Japan (the tulip) and by the strength of nature (which is also a symbol of Japan) during the storm. However, the moral principles expressed by these symbols remain in the background of the fascinating animation, fluid and complex: not only for the realistic rain, but especially the detailed movements of the spider's legs and web, which accentuate the charisma of the character and its bewitching temptation.[*]

AT THE ZENITH OF GLORY

A short animation of 1943, *Nippon banzai* by Mikami Ryōji and Nagatomi Eijirō clearly represents the Japanese war manifesto, as an article published in the *Asahi Graph* magazine on its release announced: "…here is the birth of a new style of anti-British/American PR war film. The Great Western Colonial Powers…who have committed acts of aggression against the various people of Southeast Asia are conspiring to surround and lay siege to Japan. Unable to stand by any longer, Japan begins a war, and in the wink of an eye, liberates Asia to the exaltation of the native people."[†] This movie—made with a mixture of cels, silhouettes, war photos and news reports—ridiculed the enemies, including Roosevelt and Churchill, in a realistic way.

During the last years of the war, battles and weapons were shown with greater accuracy, such as in *The War at Sea in Malaya* (*Marē okikaisen*, 1944, by Ōfuji Noburō),[‡] made on behalf of the Navy Ministry, where the real leading characters are the complex

---

[*] Historians think Masaoka was inspired by two episodes of the *Silly Symphonies* series: *The Old Mill* (1937), which opens with a ladybird flying on a spider web, and *The Spider And The Fly* (1931), where a spider attracts the insects by playing its own web as a harp.

[†] Quoted in Nornes and Fukushima (1991).

[‡] This movie is the animated equivalent of one of the greatest successes of live cinema of the same year, *The War at Sea from Hawaii to Malaya* (*Hawai Marē okikaisen*, 1942, by Yamamoto Kajirō), produced by Tōhō on behalf of the same ministry to celebrate the first anniversary of the attack on Pearl Harbor of December 7, 1941.

war machines (weapons, ships and airplanes), and human beings have irrelevant roles. Enemies were also shown in a more realistic way, even if in some cases they were represented like demons (*oni*), with horns on their heads.

Two masterpieces of cel animation, both made by Seo Mitsuyo, close the long series of war films of this period: *Momotarō's Sea Eagles* (*Momotarō no umiwashi*, 1943) and *Momotarō's Divine Sea Warriors* (*Momotarō: Umi no shinpei*, 1944). The first one was produced by the major studio Shōchiku on behalf of the Navy Ministry, again to celebrate the attack on Pearl Harbor. It was released as a feature film, but it was not, since its duration was of just 37 minutes.

Momotarō's Sea Eagles opens with the title "Dedicated to the young citizens in the greatest war of East Asia." A Japanese battleship silently sails the Pacific Ocean; on board, a crew of animals gathers to listen to their leader, Captain Momotarō (the only human on board), who announces the next mission: an air attack on Onigashima, the island of demons. When the fleet reaches the island, a massive bombing on the American battleship begins, while their crew tries to escape. Among them, the coward captain—resembling Popeye's Bluto*—tries in vain to wave a white flag, but the Japanese are relentless. The tone of the whole movie is clear from the opening scenes, when big waves from the sea seem to blend with the gray and menacing clouds. Momotarō's charisma is always stressed by the low angles used to shoot him. Only a few gags remind us that this is an animation for children.

For *Momotarō's Divine Sea Warriors*, Seo was able to count on his friend Masaoka Kenzō's cooperation.† Produced in 1944 but released on April 12, 1945, a few months before the end of the war,

---

* In the movie poster, four special enemies are sketched in the sea: Betty Boop, Popeye, Franklin Roosevelt, and Bluto.
† In particular, Masaoka is the creator of the animated silhouettes pictured in a flashback of the Portuguese invasion of Goa in the sixteenth century.

this movie contains a great amount of cels, (50,000), which confers an accurate and refined style to the animation. There are no comic scenes, and the whole atmosphere is solemn. Here again, represented as animals, Japanese officials have just completed their military training and are spending some days with their families before leaving for their mission. This part of the movie describes a bucolic countryside, a magic place of incontaminate nature. The second part of the movie is set in a Japanese colony where tigers, elephants and many other animals—representing the natives—happily learn from the colonizers several activities,* especially how to build the hangars for the Japanese fleet, which is going to depart for an attack on British headquarters.

Just as in *Momotaro's Sea Eagles*, Momotaro here represents an icon of the country, while the action is mainly performed by the group. His appearance is fundamental in the scenes where he meets the imprisoned and clumsy enemy officials and tries to get details of their strategy, since he is determined and charismatic. In the last scene, some kids are playing together, pretending to parachute into North America, an eventuality suddenly broken by the two nuclear bombs on Hiroshima and Nagasaki.

DEFEAT AND RECONSTRUCTION

The atomic bombings on Hiroshima and Nagasaki on August 6 and 9, 1945, respectively, quickened Japan's capitulation and marked the definitive end of an era. Before this tragic epilogue, the main urban centers of the country had already been reduced to rubble by the repeated air raids and the resulting fires. Not only houses but also industries, infrastructures, roads and harbors-the whole basis of the Japanese economy-had been destroyed, and the number of homeless people was growing. What was even worse,

---

* An interesting scene shows the savages who try to learn the Japanese language, emblematic of the supposed cultural supremacy of the colonizers.

the Japanese had the feeling that they had somehow lost their national identity when on August 27 the first American contingents arrived in Japan to start the seven-year occupation of the country. Paradoxically, the presence of the Allied Powers led by Americans and the following feeling of subordination meant that Japanese war culpability in the pan-Asian expansion became "softer," as Iwabuchi Kōichi notices: "…Japan was a victim, not an oppressor. While Japan as an imperial/colonial power had to seriously face the cultural and ethnic difference within the empire of the pre-war era, post-war Japan was free of this burden. It was allowed to forget its colonizing past and to become obsessed with claiming its racial purity and homogeneity through the binary opposition of two culturally organic entities, 'Japan' and 'the West'" (Iwabuchi, 2006).

Under the control of the SCAP (Supreme Commandment of the Allied Powers), the occupation forces made a huge effort to rebuild the country: on one hand, they dismantled the centers of power and assets (the industrial and financial concentrations called *zaibatsu*), and on the other hand, they introduced important social modifications, promoting the equality of rights to all the citizens, the suffrage of women and contributing to the renewal of the school system.

On September 22, 1945, the CI&E (Civil Information and Education Section) was instituted, in charge of managing the democratic propaganda. Regarding cinema, they eliminated the law of 1939, took a census of all people working in this field, and planned detailed control on productions, starting from the scripts. Only the works useful to highlight democratic values—freedom, peace, improvement of working conditions, gender and social equality—would be authorized. The ones containing militaristic, nationalistic, anti-democratic and racist elements would be forbidden. The first victims of the new laws were *jidaigeki* ("historical dramas"), since all the stories set in the past could contain one of more of the forbidden subjects. In animation, this caused the banning of *The Girl at the Dojō Temple*, which Ichikawa Kon had completed at the end of the war.*

Lastly, according to the American plans, a huge distribution of foreign movies would be the best means to easily spread democratic values, and for this reason, many animations from the United States were released, helping to raise the popularity of this art. However, in the first months of the post-war period, there was a shortage of media works,† and even mangas were barely published, since many paper factories had been destroyed. The only available entertainment was the paper theater *kamishibai*, which in this period reached its peak of popularity.

It did not take long for the first relevant turning signal to appear. In 1945, about one hundred animators, including Yamamoto Sanae, Masaoka Kenzō and Murata Yasuji, established a new production company, called New Japanese Animation (Shin Nippon Dōgasha), later renamed Society of Japanese Animation (Nihon Manga Eigasha‡). One of the first titles that they produced§ was *Cherry Blossoms* (*Sakura*, also known as *Spring Fantasy—Haru no gensō*, 1946, by Masaoka Kenzō), only distributed in 1950, because it was considered too hermetic. In black and white and without dialogue, inspired by the brilliant *Invitation to the Dance* by Carl Maria von Weber, this movie focuses on two fairy butterflies flying gracefully, with the transparency of their wings crossing cherry petals blown by the wind through a detailed filmic

---

* For a long time, lost and found only at the beginning of the new century, this movie— a live action with *bunraku* puppets—adapted a classic kabuki play: a young woman, Kiyohime, falls in love with the monk Anchin, but he refuses her and she transforms herself into a snake to harass him. In Ichikawa's version, the woman sacrifices herself in the end to help Anchin complete the construction of a big bell.

† In 1945, from the beginning of the occupation, only the short animation *Insect Kingdom* (*Konchū tengoku*, by Suzuki Hiromasa) was released in Japan.

‡ The words *manga eiga* (cinema of manga) were first used with the meaning of animation by the critic Imamura Taihei in 1948 in his essay *On Cartoons* (*Manga eiga ron*).

§ The produced movies were distributed by the major studio Tōhō. From 1948, Tōhō also launched its own department of animation called Tōhō Educational Movies Company (*Tōhō Kyōiku Eiga Kabushikigaisha*).

grammar (extreme angles, fluid change of plans, and so on). Like in Disney's *Fantasia*, trees, human beings, animals and the passing of seasons are equal protagonists of an idyllic fresco, where there is no sign of the recent war.

Under the direction of Murata Yasuji, the Nihon Manga Eigasha produced *The King's Tail* (*Ōsama no shippo*, 1949, by Seo Mitsuyo), an adaptation of Andersen's *The Emperor's New Clothes*. The prince of foxes was born with no tail, but everybody is forced to pretend to see it. In the beginning, a big budget was projected, but because of some economic difficulties, the production came to a standstill many times and the final duration was reduced from 47 to 33 minutes. In addition, even if the filmmaker had selected this subject considering it a democratic example, Tōhō managers believed that it was too leftist (they labeled it *aka*, "red") and stopped the distribution. Disappointed by this experience, Seo abandoned animation and spent the rest of his life as an illustrator of books for children.

In 1947, Masaoka, Yamamoto Sanae and other animators left the Nihon Manga Eigasha and founded the new Japan Animated Film (Nihon Dōga Eiga)—later shortened to Nichidō Eiga—which became part of the major studio Tōei Dōga in 1956. Masaoka made one of his most famous movies, the musical *Abandoned Cat Little Tora* (*Suteneko Torachan*, 1947), followed one year later by *Tora-chan and the Bride* (*Torachan no hanayome*) and in 1949 by the last episode, *Tora-chan and the Cancan Bug* (*Torachan no kankan mushi*). "*Tora*" (which in Japanese means "tiger") is an orphan kitten adopted by a lonely mother cat with three kids, but the youngest one, Miike, is jealous of him*—orphans and widows were tragically numerous in this period. The movie opens and closes with the same scene, that is, showing the four kittens happily playing near a Christmas tree (the story is told in a flashback)—which is, together with the sunflowers in the field where Tora is found, a Western symbol. After the success of these movies, Masaoka

---

* In the following episodes, Miike is a co-protagonist with Tora.

retired from animation because of his eye problems and became a teacher, even though he always hoped to make a last movie by adapting *The Little Mermaid*.

POSTWAR "ANIMATES"

Various sources report *Princess of Baghdad* (*Bagudaddo hime*, 1948, by Suzuki Hiromasa*) as being the first animated movie of the postwar period; however, others had been produced in 1946, as the title *Cherry Blossoms* demonstrates. Many films were aimed to instill a sense of faith in the reconstruction through Western cooperation, such as *Magic Pen* (*Mahō no pen*, 1946, by Kumagawa Masao†) the story of an orphan who finds a Western doll among the ruins, takes it home and repairs it. In a dream, the doll comes to life, greets him in English and gives him a magic pen that can create anything he desires. The boy uses it to rebuild his own house and the destroyed city, and even if this is only a dream, it embodies the hope of the whole country—thanks to the American support, as the English short dialogue suggests.

Tora's adventures and *Magic Pen* are not the only movies dedicated to orphans, who made up a huge portion of the population and were seen as innocent victims of the faults of their parents. Among the numerous films, some are an adaptation of the famous tale *The Little Match Girl* by Andersen; examples are the two silhouette movies of 1947, *The Little Match Girl* (*Macchi uri no shōjo* by Yamamoto Sanae) and the delicate *Dream of a Snowy Night* (*Yuki no yoru no yume* by Ōfuji Noburō).

---

* As a matter of fact, it was the first feature film. Among the sources which gave the incorrect information about it, an article in the *Japan Times* on February 23, announcing the restoration of the print. See http://www.japantimes.co.jp/news/2006/02/23/news/first-postwar-animated-film-returns/#.UdFMmhZif2w.

† The script of this movie was by Susukita Rokuhei, who had been the scriptwriter of one of the most liberal live-action movies of the 1920s, *The Serpent* (*Orochi*, 1925), directed by Futagawa Buntarō. This movie blended local traditional elements into the foreign story, as in the reference to the tenth century Japanese story, *The Tale of the Bamboo Cutter* (*Taketori monogatari*) in the magical elements used in the scenes, in which the princess is a point of contention for some pretenders.

Not only Western tales were adapted to the screen, but also many traditional Japanese short novels became favorite subjects in animation, such as *The Spider's Thread* (*Kumo no ito*, 1946, by Ōfuji Noburō, which received an award at the Uruguay Film Festival), adapted from the same short novel that would later inspire the famous *Rashōmon* (1950) by Kurosawa Akira. This is the story of a merciless criminal who feels compassion for a spider that he decides not to kill. When the man dies and falls down to the underworld, the spider tries to help him, sending down a thread of its web, but when the man tries to climb it, the other damned people also follow him, and the thread breaks. Often adapted in animation, this story of Buddhist compassion and human greed is a symbol of the everyday struggle of people.

Occupation forces also incentivized the sport genre and particularly those movies that contained baseball. Examples are *My Baseball* (*Boku no yakyū*, 1948, by Asano Megumi, the first color Japanese animation) and *Animal Great Baseball Battle* (*Dōbutsu dai yakyū sen*, 1949, by Yamamoto Sanae). Other sports were also presented, such as horse racing in *Sport of Little Tanuki* (*Supōtsu kotanuki*, 1949, by Furusawa Hideo). Also, musicals were incentivized, and many titles were very successful, such as *The Bear Dodger* (*Kuma ni kuwarenu otoko*, 1948, by Ōfuji Noburō), one of the first approved *jidaigekis*.* Two men are traveling together and one of them hurts a little bear. When the animal's father rushes to its aid, the cowardly man escapes, leaving his travel mate alone to deal with the situation. This movie also represents a good example of the new and strongly approved *kyōiku eiga* ("educational films"), since they could easily teach socially correct behaviors to young people.†

---

* As clearly indicated in the opening titles, this is a *chonmage manga*: *chonmage* is the particular hairstyle of samurais, thus the word means "manga set in the past" with contemporary elements.

† Among others, *Poppoyasan: The Good-for-Nothing Station Master* (*Poppoyasan: Nonkina ekichō no maki*, 1948, by Kumakawa Masao), which teaches the correct safety regulations to be followed at railway stations.

In the fervid climate of innovation, however, the democratization of the country soon showed its first rifts. The Occupation Powers had approved the intervention of labor unions in the cinema organizations, considering the possible debates as a guarantee for social stability. Labor unions arose for the first time inside the majors. In the beginning of 1946, they were all gathered in the All Japan Film Employees Association (*Zen Nippon eiga jugyoin kumiai domei*, shortened to *Zen'ei*), which a month later was given the name of All Japan Motion Picture and Drama Employees Union (*Zen Nippon Eiga Engeki Jugyoin Kumiai Domei*, shortened to *Nichien'ei*), also in charge of enlisting the names of war criminals. However, not all requests by the Union were accepted, finding the major studio Tōhō particularly unfavorable, where, from the end of 1946, a series of strikes began. In August 1947, the studios were occupied and saved by the huge intervention of both Japanese police and the occupation's army.

The political climate was quickly changing, and in the time span of a few years (1947–1951), Japan was involved in the fury of the red purge (*reddo pāji*). The Communist Party was suppressed and thousands of people, including 137 working in cinema, were stigmatized as being "red" and lost their jobs. The peak of persecution was reached on June 6, 1950, when the *Official Gazette* (*Kanpo* vol. 58*) published a directive from General MacArthur to Prime Minister Yoshida Shigeru, asking him to "purge" the twenty-four main members of the Communist Party's central committee, accused of opposing the democracy. Meanwhile, some of those who had been judged as war criminals in the first witch hunt were now reintegrated into their previous positions.

---

* The integral directive is available at the link: http://www.ndl.go.jp/modern/e/img_r/M009/M009-001r.html. This letter followed an event that happened on May 30, when a group of Communist demonstrators erupted during a celebration of the American holiday, Memorial Day. Some American soldiers were injured and eight protesters were arrested (Dower, 2000).

A PERSONAL VIEW: ŌFUJI NOBURŌ'S INTERNATIONAL HITS

Ōfuji Noburō was very active in the postwar period. Until his death in 1961, he made almost a movie a year, with a peak of four titles in 1952. Occupation forces never censored his work. As Ōfuji himself explained in his essay of 1956, *30 Years of Silhouette Film* (*Kage e eiga sanjū nen**), an American official had loved his movies such as *Spider's Thread*, and for this reason, his films did not incur censorship. Besides, they contained many Western elements together with the Japanese traditional ones, especially some Buddhist themes (starting from the short *Buddha—Shaka*, 1948†).

Many of his movies were screened at international film festivals, and particularly, the animations addressed to the adult audience were highly appreciated, both in Japan and abroad.

In 1952, the filmmaker completed a color remake of his own *Whale* of 1927, which he presented one year later at the Cannes Film Festival, where it was admired by the president of the jury, Jean Cocteau, and by a special spectator, Pablo Picasso. Ōfuji used black silhouettes for the characters and cut cels for the background, overlapping the images by means of a multiplane stand to obtain elaborate nuances and special effects, especially in the scenes showing the fury of the storm on the sea.

Although in this period Ōfuji also made animations for children, such as *Flower and Butterfly* (*Hana to chō*, 1954), his best films were intended for adults. In 1956, his *Ghost Ship* (*Yūreisen*), a complex work, again dedicated to human power and sexual yearning received an award at the Venice Film Festival. Like in *Whale*, the overlapping of images by means of multiplane animation confers suggestive effects of transparency. Here again, evil—a

---

* Tokyo, Japan, Geijutsu Shinchō, p. 232.
† This was his most ambitious work: after this first part, he went on working on the same project, unfortunately released after his death in 1961 in a shorter version, with the title *Life of Buddha* (*Shaka no shōgai*). Other titles related to spirituality are *Adam and Eve* (*Seisho gensōfu Adamu to Ibu*, 1951) and *The Venerable Shakyamuni* (*Taisei Shakuson*, 1952).

pirate ship and its crew—is represented through black silhouettes. Pirates assault a ship, rape the women and kill all passengers. While sailing, they meet the same ship once again, which has now become a ghost vessel: it is white, representing a symbol of *onryō* (the "revengeful phantoms"). As in the best horror tradition, phantoms do not physically assault the pirates but drive them crazy to the point that they kill each other, and at the end, a big eye (seeing is one of the main tools of the emotional repertoire of horror) swallows the last man.

Between 1955 and 1959, Ōfuji made five movies starting with the title *Story of Kojiki* (*Kojiki monogatari*)—dedicated to some of the events described in the oldest mythologic sources of Japanese literature (*Kojiki* was completed in approximately 712).

After his death, the Mainichi Film Concours established the Ōfuji Noburō Award, annually conferred to animators who distinguish themselves with excellence and innovation in animated cinema. The first filmmaker to get the prize was Tezuka Osamu, followed by authors known today and loved throughout the world, such as Okamoto Tadanari, Kawamoto Kihachirō, Kuri Yōji, Miyazaki Hayao, Ōtomo Katsuhiro and Kon Satoshi.

THE TURNING POINT

The Treaty of San Francisco in 1951 marked the end of the Allied Powers occupation of Japan (excluding Okinawa), which came into force on April 28, 1952. The last seven years as a whole had economically and morally blown the country down. As Dower notices, "…the occupation of the defeated nation began in August 1945 and ended in April 1952, six years and eight months later, almost twice as long as the war itself. In those years, Japan had no sovereignty and accordingly no diplomatic relations. No Japanese were allowed to travel abroad until the occupation was almost over; no major political, administrative or economic decisions were possible without the conquerors' approval; no public criticism of the American regime was permissible, although in the end dissident voices were irrepressible."*

Even if the country was exhausted, the dream of an artistic autonomy drove many animators who had taken shelter abroad to return to Japan. In 1953, the father of puppet animation Mochinaga Tadahito (1919–1999, also known as Mochinaga Tad) returned from China. He had spent his youth in Manchuria. He then returned to Japan to study at university and started working on animation by cooperating with Seo Mitsuyo at the Geijutsu Eigasha. He planned and built a four-level multiplane stand to create interesting three-dimensional effects for Seo's short movie *Ant Boy* (*Ari chan*, 1941). In 1944, Mochinaga made his debut as a filmmaker with *Fuku-chan's Submarine* (*Fuku chan no sensuikan*, 1944), and later, after cooperating with Seo for *Momotarō's Sea Eagles*, he went back to Manchuria to supervise the Japanese-controlled *Man'ei* (*Manchū Eiga*, "Manchurian Studios").

After Japan's defeat, Mochinaga further improved his techniques, working with Chinese staff on the first stop motion of both China and Japan, *The Emperor's Dreams* (*Kōtei no yume*, 1947). The following year, with the name Fan Ming, he made his first all-cel movie, *A Turtle in the Pot* (*Kame no naka de toraerareta kame*). He also cooperated in the foundation of Shanghai Animation Studios before going back to Japan in 1953.

In the same year, the NHK (*Nippon Hōsō Kyōkai*, Japan Broadcasting Corporation) began to broadcast its television programs; Mochinaga soon produced commercials for Asahi Beer, later collected with the overall title *Beer, Those Were the Days* (*Bīru mukashi mukashi*, 1956, a series that also included an episode by Ōfuji Noburō). Together with other animators, he founded the Art Puppets Production (*Ningyō Geijutsu* Production), and from 1955, he made several shorts in stop motion, including

---

* Moreover, the news related to the numerous rapes, murders and thefts perpetuated by the occupation soldiers to the detriment of Japanese people were forbidden (Dower, 2000, p. 23).

Princess Tsumeko and Amanojaku (*Tsumeko hime to Amanojaku*, 1955). The first episode of his series dedicated to the *Little Black Sambo* (*Chibikuro Sanbo*, after Helen Bannerman's character) was awarded as best movie for children at the Vancouver International Film Festival. On this occasion, he met Arthur Rankin and later cooperated with Videocraft International, after establishing his own MOM Film Studios.

While television broadcast was contributing to unify the country, a massive immigration—especially of Koreans—made Japanese people face a problem of cultural homogeneity. Moreover, a huge inflow of people from the countryside to the cities was creating a gap between rural and urban realities. In this atmosphere of contrasts, a kind of connective tissue among people was represented by consumerism, widespread in the country through the so-called *masukomi*, ("mass communication"). Many television programs from the United States contributed to creating a new style of life for the middle class, and electronics and cars especially became the cornerstone of desire,* even if the new models did not compensate for the element of criticism toward American culture and a sense of resentment for the recent nuclear bombing. With the end of the occupation, for the first time it was possible to clearly refer to the tragedy and to the many *hibakusha* (the surviving victims). The fear of an atomic tragedy newly surfaced because of the risk of a third bombing on North Korea, and especially after the Daigo Fukuryū Maru incident, when a Japanese fishing boat was exposed and contaminated by a nuclear test by Americans in the Bikini Atoll on March 1, 1954.

Several animated films were dedicated to this subject in the following decades, but the first movie to clearly denounce the nuclear attack in an animated style was not a real animation, but the

---

* During the 1950s, desire coincided with the three Ss—*senpuki, sentakuki suihanki*: electric fan, washing machine, and electric kettle. In the 1960s, it was the three Cs (for the English words *car, cooler* and *color television*), and in the 1970s, the three Js (*jūero, jetto* e *jūtaku* for jewels, jet and private home).

famous *Godzilla* (*Gojira*, 1954, by Honda Ishirō)—in which the monster is generated by thermonuclear experiments. A pioneer of *kaijū eiga* ("monster films"), this movie was made with the contribution of the special effects (strongly influenced by the American *King Kong*) by Tsuburaya Eiji* who had already created the effects of the most famous war movie of the war period: *The War at Sea from Hawaii to Malaya.*

---

* Tsuburaya experimented with the "suitmotion" animation for the Godzilla character (an actor wearing a costume and moving into a miniature town), also using a storyboard for the first time in Japan.

CHAPTER 3

A New World

I N JAPAN, EXPERIMENTAL CINEMA (*jikken eiga*, before the war
called "avant-garde cinema," *zen'ei eiga*) found new impetus in
the postwar period, relaunched by the poet and critic Takiguchi
Shūzō, a friend of André Breton and Marcel Duchamp, who in
1947 presented the works of Maya Deren and John and James
Whitney (Nishijima, 1994) through his articles. Together with
other artists, including music composer Takemitsu Tōru, in 1951
he established the Experimental Laboratory (*Jikken Kōbō*), where
Ōtsuji Seiji, Tsuji Saiko and Ishimoto Yasuhiro made the first
abstract animation of the period, *Kine Calligraph*.

The 1950s paved the way for many artistic experiments, intended
to define the specificity of each form of art (cinema, literature,
painting, music and theater), blending them together, so as to
create new ways of expression. Together with Jikken Kōbō, The
Century Association (*Seiki no kai*, launched in 1948) was one of
the most important associations of the period, which included
among its members some of the most important artists of the
following years: Takemitsu Tōru, the novelist Abe Kōbō and

the filmmaker Teshigahara Hiroshi.* In addition, Teshigahara, son of the founder of the Sōgetsu ikebana school, contributed to the founding of the Sōgetsu Art Museum (*Sōgetsu Bijutsukan*) inside the Sōgetsu Kaikan building, which from 1958 hosted many cultural discussions and experimental activities—animation, dance, theater, music and even television programs, including those of foreign artists John Cage and David Tudor and animators Norman McLaren and Jiří Trnka. From 1960 to 1964, the center also published the magazine *SAC* (*Sōgetsu Art Centre*, later renamed *Sac Journal*), presenting its activities and essays on the artists.

In this tsunami of inventions, in 1958, animator Kuri Yōji, illustrator Yanagihara Ryōhei and painter Manabe Hiroshi founded the Animation Group of Three (*Animēshon sannin no kai*) with the aim of making and promoting art movies. From 1960, they also started a festival of animation at the Sōgetsu Kaikan, opening the first edition with their own works and presenting a manifesto of intents: they disagreed with those who refused foreign influences and at the same time stigmatized those who were not able to create something originally subjective and free from any restriction.

Yanagihara Ryōhei was the most traditional of the three, both in his graphic and filmmaking style. He had been an advertiser for Suntory, where, for one year, he also directed the magazine *Paradise of Whiskey* (*Yoshu tengoku*). From 1958, he made some animated commercials for Suntory by using the character Uncle Torys. When he joined Manabe and Kuri, he began working on animation for adults, showing from his first film *Sea Battle* (*Kaisen*, 1960) his interest in social satire and psychological in-depth study of characters, as Yanagihara himself declared during the presentation of his *Female—The Strange Story of Yonosuke* (*Onna—Yonosuke ibun*, 1963): "In terms of animation it is difficult to portray the minimal movements in the psychological expressions of the Japanese. With *Onna*, I wanted to see how I could express this

---

* Teshigahara and Abe made four live action movies together, including *Woman in the Dunes* (*Suna no onna*, 1964), which received an award at the Cannes Film Festival.

mind's dynamic impressions of everyday people in an interesting way" (Nishijima, 1994). Yanagihara's career as an animator was brief, since he returned to his previous job as an illustrator after his last short movie, *The Baikal Ship* (*Baikaru maru*, 1966).

Manabe Hiroshi's experience in animation lasted only from 1960 to 1966. He had been a well-known book illustrator, especially the science fiction novels by Hoshi Shin'ichi and thrillers by Agatha Christie and Edogawa Ranpo. His retro-futuristic style combined brilliant colors, which reminded one of pop art and peculiar forms painted on huge surfaces. His first animation, *Animation for a Stage* (*Butai no tame no animēshon*, 1960), was presented at the first edition of the Sōgetsu festival. Among his experiments, his next work *Cine poem n. 1* (1962) shows the image of a woman who is first filtered by a kaleidoscope, then split and recreated. By parceling out every part of her body—which takes on a life of its own—the author suggests the unreality of human beings.

Considered as Manabe's best animation, *Submarine Cassiopea* (*Sensuikan Cashiopea*, 1964) is a mix between live cinema, drawings, silhouettes and light effects: the leading character is water, which is able to subsume and transform anything—metamorphoses by means of this liquid symbolize the extent to which our subjectivity may convey a wrong perception of the world. The following *Chase* (*Tsuiseki*, 1966) was his last animation; however, Manabe was considered a renowned painter until his death in 2000.

Of the three animators, Kuri Yōji (nom de plume of Kurihara Hideo) is the most famous and innovative. He was also internationally awarded and appreciated. During his career, he produced hundreds of works: movies, commercials, paintings, sculptures, stage scenarios and even mangas. Kuri had been a pupil of Ōfuji Noburō's before beginning his studies at the prestigious Bunka Gakuin Art School, during which he worked as a cartoonist and a painter. In 1955, he made his first animation, a commercial for Mitsua Soup Company.

After launching the Animation Group of Three, in 1961, he established his own Kuri's Laboratory of Experimental Manga

(*Kuri Jikken Manga Kōbō*) and produced his movies addressed to an adult audience. *Two Grilled Fish* (*Nihiki no sanma*), *Fantasia of Stamps* (*Kitte no gensō*) and *Human Zoo* (*Ningen dōbutsuen*) are only the first examples of his peculiar style, where fixed images alternate to dynamic scenes, showing extreme metamorphoses. Rough graphics, often interchanged with other techniques (such as silhouettes and pixelation), combine with experiments in sound and color.* The stories always concern his contemporary insane world and the violence that permeates it, for example, by means of technology (such as in the anti-nuclear *Two Grilled Fish*). Above all, they are related to the battle of the sexes accentuated by female emancipation, such as in *Human Zoo*, where some women abuse men held in cages.† To describe this conflict, Kuri resorts to extreme images (including pornography and physiological functions) and to paradox. In *Love* (*Ai*, 1963, which received an award at the Venice Film Festival, just like *Human Zoo*), the leading woman who finds and enslaves a man that is rude, selfish, sadistic and physically enormous. Not even Kuri sympathizes with men, who are weak, masturbators and inclined to war and also have a marginal role in procreating (like in the surreal *The Eggs of Sado—Sado no tamago*, 1966).‡ Kuri's works were inevitably classified as scandalous, in particular the erotic *Aos* (1964, which also received an award at the Oberhausen Festival), graphically inspired by Hieronymus Bosch and based on the manga by Inoue Yōsuke,§ accompanied by a particular soundtrack made of sexual moans performed by the artist Yoko Ono.

---

* One of the best titles is *Au Fou!* (1968), a collage of caustic and irreverent gags whose rhythm is given by the soundtrack.

† Kuri makes peculiar use of space, which gives a strong sense of claustrophobia. This is more evident in *The Room* (*Heya*, 1967, which also received an award at the Venice Film Festival), which also displays the theme of human voyeurism—people and objects in a cubic structure observed as if they were on a stage.

‡ They are often losers, for example, in *Samurai* (1965): on a plane, two men fight for a woman, but she eats both of them, realizing soon after that she has lost the only two people for whom she was important.

§ Inoue also presented the screening at Sōgetsu Kaikan in 1964.

SŌGETSU KAIKAN: FERMENT OF INDEPENDENCE

In an interview released in the 1980s, Tezuka Osamu argued: "After the appearance of Mr. Kuri and a lot of artists at the Sōgetsu Art Festival I felt relieved because I thought they could take charge of the Japanese animation world."* The works by the three animators represented a turning point in the overall production, especially by demonstrating that it was possible to be free from European and American influences, so as to create personal stylistic paths.

Together with the annual animation festival by the three animators (1960–1964), in 1961, the Sōgetsu Center also launched a film library, where every year many experimental films and documentaries were screened. In 1966, the International Avant-Garde Film Festival directed by Henri Lanlois (expressly invited by the *Cinémathèque Française*)† was established, after the new *Animation Festival 65* had been launched the previous year. Many filmmakers had various chances to show their works, including Yokoo Tadanori, one of the most internationally acclaimed artists, considered the precursor of Japanese pop art,‡ who was the creator of three animations: *Kiss kiss kiss* (1964), *The Creaking Mountain—Couples' Precepts* (*Kachikachi yama meoto no sujimichi*, 1964) and *Privileged Images* (*Tokuten eizō*, 1965), all presented at the Sōgetsu Kaikan. In these works, Yokoo examines the main fetishistic and psychotropic icons of the period, edited with different rhythms according to the signs they embedded in society: images of kisses, which dissolve one into the other, thus becoming meaningless; popular stars of the period (such as Brigitte Bardot, Alain Delon, Elizabeth Taylor, Richard Burton, The Beatles and Marilyn Monroe) alternated with Coca Cola, airplanes, film genre icons and so on.

---

* Available at the link: https://www.dailymotion.com/video/xb5zqb.
† A detailed chronology of Sōgetsu Kaikan's activities is available at the link: http://www.sogetsu.or.jp/e/know/successive/artcenter/activity.html.
‡ Because of his psychedelic style—through which he revisits the traditional arts of his country—Yokoo has been reductively defined as the "Japanese Warhol."

With these three movies and his painting works, as Jelena Stojikovic highlights: "Yokoo not only explored innovative graphic design styles but also announced final inclusion of Japan into international art circles of the postmodern, globalized era" (Stojikovic, 2010). The works by Tsukioka Sadao were also presented at Sōgetsu Kaikan. He had become an independent animator in 1964* when he directed the short movie *Cigarettes and Ashes* (*Tabako to hai*, 1965) for Tezuka Osamu's Mushi Production, screened at the *Animation Festival 65*, followed by *The Story of a Man* (*Aru otoko no baai*, 1966). In 1965, together with Hayashi Seiichi, he launched the KnacK Productions (later renamed Ichi Corporation), where he made *The Creation—New Version* (*Shin Tenchi sōzō*, 1970, which received an award at the Cracovia Film Festival), all presented at Sōgetsu.

Just as in the case of Tsukioka deriving from Tōei (we will refer to the major in the following pages), Shimamura Tatsuo made surreal independent animations, all presented at Sōgetsu Kaikan and related to human existence and solitude in labyrinthine environments: *Moonlight and the Glasses* (*Tsukiyo to megane*, 1966), *Illusion City* (*Gen'ei toshi*, 1967) and *The Invisible Man* (*Tōmei ningen*, 1968).†

Produced while working at Kuri's Laboratory, Furukawa Taku also presented his debut work at the Sōgetsu Kaikan, *Red Dragonfly* (*Akatombo*, 1966). This animation was strongly influenced by McLaren and Kuri themselves and was followed by about twenty short movies, mainly produced by Kuri's own company Takun Manga Box, founded in 1968. Characterized by his personal and visionary style, his best works of the 1970s were related to the study of movement (*Phenakistiscope—Odorokihan*, 1975, which received an award at Annecy), to the exploration of an oneiric universe (*The Beautiful Planet—Utsukushii shiisei*), and

---

* Tsukioka had collaborated with Tezuka Osamu before working on many feature films and TV series produced at Tōei, where he had also launched the TV series *Ken The Wolf Boy* (*Ōkami Shōnen Ken*, 1963–1965) together with Takahata Isao.
† He later abandoned filmmaking to dedicate himself entirely to special effects and computer animation produced by his Shirogumi Studio, founded in 1974.

to dark tales (*Cow's Head—Ushi atama*, about a man with a cow's head who terrorizes a village with an axe). Abstract figures and comic-like images alternate, sometimes becoming minimalist lines moving with an extraordinary dynamic effect (especially in *Speed* of 1980, which received the Ōfuji Noburō Award).

Besides Sōgetsu Kaikan, in the same years, many other associations dedicated to animation made their debut, including the Association of Animation (*Animēshon Dōkōkai*, better known by the diminutive Anidō), founded in 1967 with the purpose of doing "research and interchange for the creation of professional animators...[organizing] many kinds of screenings and workshops...publishing books about animation, collecting 16 mm films and the materials for any category of animation, and distributing new animation films in the world."*

THE BIRTH OF TŌEI

Ōkawa Hiroshi, an experienced businessman, took the helm of a new company as its president: using the revenue of Tōyoko Railway, in 1951, the major studio Tōei (*Tōei Kabushikigaisha*) was launched, also incorporating the little Tōyoko Eiga (whose chief became the director of the new company) and Ōizumi Eiga Productions. From 1956, Tōei also acquired the Nihon Dōga, inaugurating the Tōei Animation Company (*Tōei Dōga Kabushikigaisha*, later renamed *Tōei Animēshon Kabushikigaisha*).

One of the main purposes of the new company was to produce high-level feature animations tantamount to Disney's classic movies. As a first step, a few shorts were made to test the quality, including *Kitty's Graffiti* (*Koneko no rakugaki*, 1957), co-directed by Yabushita Taiji† and Mori Yasuji—the story of a kitten that

---

* http://www.anido.com/about?lang=en.
† (1903–1986), Yabushita graduated in photography before entering the major studio Shōchiku and, later, the Ministry of Education as a documentarist. After the war, he joined the Nippon Dōga and debuted as an animator with *The Story of the Little Rabbit* (*Kousagi monogatari*, 1952). When Nippon Dōga was incorporated in Tōei Dōga, Yabushita became its director.

scribbles on a wall some drawings that begin to move—fluidly animated through line drawings (*senga*) and cels, with a rhythmic editing and the images horizontally flowing like in ancient handscrolls.

Tōei Dōga's first feature film was released in 1958: *Panda and the Magic Serpent* (*Hakujaden*, which received an award at the Venice Children's Film Festival in 1959) by Yabushita Taiji and Ōkabe Kazuhiko, was based on a Hong Kong legend, even if it contained many traditional Japanese elements.* Together with the abundance of musical scenes, this movie followed the Disney classic practice of presenting pretty animals, in this case the panda and *tanuki* (symbols of China and Japan, respectively), as friends of the leading character, a young boy.

The second feature film, which was also the first to be produced in CinemaScope in Japan, was *Magic Boy* (*Shōnen Sarutobi Sasuke*, 1959, lit. *The Boy Sarutobi Sasuke*†), co-directed by Yabushita and Daikubara Akira, with Yamamoto Sanae's artistic supervision. It tells the story of a young boy in medieval Japan who learns the art of *ninjutsu* (used by *ninjas*) to defeat Princess Yasha, the perfidious demon who is threatening people. In these first movies, all the characters have Japanese features, and Yasha especially aesthetically resembles the old ukiyo-e print demons, performing a metamorphosis typical of the kabuki plays.

The following work, *Alakazam the Great* (*Saiyuki*, lit. *Journey to the West*, 1960), refers to an old Chinese novel of the sixteenth century, telling the story of a young monk who is traveling from China to India, taking some Buddhist sutras. Along with him are a pig, another monk and the monkey Songoku—the leading character in this movie, here described as an arrogant animal—which had

---

* This is the love story between a boy, Hu Hsien, and a young girl, Pai Niang (who is the reincarnation of the white serpent he had owned when he was a child), and of the monk Fa Hai, who believes she is an evil spirit and tries to separate them.
† The American distributor Metro Goldwyn Mayer preferred changing the original title to *The Adventures of the Little Samurai*, since a samurai had a positive appeal, while ninjas were considered spies and killers.

already been the protagonist of other animations.* From 1952, it had also been the leading character of a series of mangas by Tezuka Osamu entitled *Songoku the Monkey* (*Boku no Songoku*), from which the movie also takes inspiration. There was a ploy to add Tezuka's name among the credits with co-directors Yabushita Taiji and Shirakawa Daisuke—even if he had worked only on the script. However, Tezuka disagreed with the choice of a happy ending (on the line of Disney's productions) and preferred Songoku's death, the main reason why he suspended his cooperation with the major.†

Together with Serikawa Yūgo, in 1961, Yabushita directed a new adaptation from the Japanese novel by Mori Ōgai *Sanshō The Bailiff* (*Sanshō dayū*, already adapted into a live action movie with the same title by Mizoguchi Kenji in 1954). Entitled *Anju and Zushiōmaru* (*Anju to Zushiōmaru*, distributed as *The Littlest Warrior*), it is the sad story of a young brother and sister who had been separated by their mother to be sold to the cruel bailiff Sanshō. Unlike the previous optimistic movies, in this film many shadows and a tragic destiny cross the lives of the two orphans. After this, the major mostly produced movies with traditional Japanese plots and contents, such as *Doggie March* (*Wanwan Chūshingura*, 1963, based on an original story by Tezuka‡) and *The Little Prince and the Eight-Headed Dragon* (*Wanpaku ōji no orochi taiji*, lit: *The Naughty Prince's Orochi Slaying*, 1963, by Serikawa Yūgo§), based on *The Chronicles of Japan* (*Nihon shoki*, completed in 720), the oldest mythological history of Japan.

---

* Among others, *The Story of Songoku* (*Saiyuki Songoku monogatari*, 1926) by Ōfuji Noburō.
† For all references, refer to Tezuka's works at http://tezukaosamu.net/en/anime/2.html. Despite this conflict, Tezuka later cooperated with the major working on the script of another feature film, *Arabian Nights: The Adventures of Sinbad* (*Arabian naito: Sindobaddo no bōken*, 1962, co-directed by Yabushita and Kuroda Masao).
‡ This is the first job as in-betweener for the young Miyazaki Hayao.
§ For the first time in the production of this film, a director of animation—here Mori Yasuji—was assigned, so as to give fluidity and a uniform style to the scenes. The movie also received the Ōfuji Noburō Award.

During the 1960s, the production of feature animated films at Tōei decreased, while the major intensified production of the series to be broadcast on television. However, a few movies were entrusted by President Ōkawa Hiroshi to a group of animators who had trained at Tōei, including Takahata Isao and Miyazaki Hayao. Some of the titles were failures, as in the case of *Gulliver's Space Travels* (*Garibā no uchū no ryōko*, 1965, by Kuroda Yoshio), the first movie with Western atmospheres supposedly destined for international distribution. Sometimes, there were not enough staff members to guarantee a good animation. This was the case of *Jack and the Witch* (*Shōnen Jakku to mahōtsukai*, 1967, by Yabushita Taiji), not perfectly animated despite the good narrative structure and the fascinating abstract backgrounds in the *Beowulf* style made by painter Koyama Reiji. An even worse result was *The World of Hans Christian Andersen* (*Anderusen monogatari*, 1968, by Yabuki Kimio), completely failing to emulate Disney's style.

A high-quality standard of animation was reached by the debut movie by Takahata Isao. *The Great Adventure of Horus* (*Taiyō no ōji—Horusu no daiboken*, 1968) tells the story of a young boy who tries to defeat the demon Grunwald, who threatens the village where he was born, from which he escaped with his father when he was a little child. To hinder the boy's mission, a mysterious girl named Hilda and the villagers themselves hinder the boy's mission. The director of animation was Ōtsuka Yasuo, while Miyazaki Hayao worked on the layouts and backgrounds and Mori Yasuji on the features of some characters. The film was based on an old bunraku drama by Fukazawa Kazuo entitled *The Sun of Chikisani* (*Chikisani no taiyō*), telling of the Ainus, the first oppressed ethnic group of Japan; Takahata and his colleagues were interested in the social motivations that led to their oppression. However, the major disapproved of their choice to the point that they had to pretend that the story took place in a village in Scandinavia; nevertheless, they succeeded in giving a strong political impact to the story, since all the characters were described as existing at a similar level, with no hierarchical priority, a group suffering from oppression: human fragility and imperfection of feelings are highlighted, and thus, the story is without heroes. Despite its innovative style, this movie was considered a failure by the major. The next direction one year later was assigned to Yabuki Kimio, titled *The Wonderful World of Puss 'n Boots* (*Nagagutsu o haita neko*). It adapted Perrault's tale,* with rich backdrops and a high entertainment level, becoming a hit, soon followed by two sequels.† It was considered a kind of recipe for success, and thus, the following works were almost all based on Western tales for children: in 1970, there was *Little Remi and Famous Dog Kapi* (*Chibikko Remi to meiken Kapi*, from Malot's *Nobody's Boy*, directed by Serikawa Yūgo) and then *Twenty Thousand Leagues Under the Sea* (*Kaitei sanmai mairu*, 1971, by Tamiya Takeshi from a manga by Ishinomori Shōtarō). Stevenson's *Treasure Island* inspired *Animal Treasure Island* (*Dōbutsu takarajima*, 1971, by Ikeda Hiroshi, with the animations, among others, by Miyazaki Hayao); *Ali Baba and the Forty Thieves* (*Aribaba to yonjūppiki no tōzoku*, 1971, by Shidara Hiroshi) was a sequel to the famous folk tale; and, there were also adaptations from Andersen's *The Little Mermaid*, like in *Andersen Story Mermaid Princess* (*Andersen monogatari ningyō hime*, 1975, by Katsumata Tomoharu).

However, not all these productions reached high-quality levels at Tōei. The best result in years only arrived in 1979, when the filmmaker Urayama Kirio‡ adapted a short novel by Matsutani Miyoko to the big screen, *Tarō the Dragon Boy* (*Tatsu no ko Tarō*). Tarō is a young boy who discovers that his long-missed mother

---

* From the Japanese version of Perrault's name, Pero, the name of the leading character, was chosen, whose image has been used as the logo of the major ever since.

† *Ringo Rides West* (*Nagagutsu sanjūshi*, lit. *Cavalier Booted Three Musketeers*, 1972, by Katsumata Tomoharu) and *Puss n' Boots: Around the World in 80 Days* (*Nagagutsu o haita neko: Hachi jū nichikan sekai isshū*, 1976, by Shidara Hiroshi).

‡ Urayama used to be a live action filmmaker, widely acclaimed especially for his debut film *Foundry Town* (*Kyupora no aru machi*, 1962).

has been transformed into a dragon and travels to a distant land to find her, helped by a magical potion that he gets from a *tengu*, due to which he becomes strong and invincible. From the opening scenes, this film reveals itself to be mature and complex, especially in its themes. The boy's true mission is to quickly pass through his childhood to become a responsible adult; solidarity and equality create strength; and compassion helps transform monsters into human beings. Thanks to the traditional pictorial style, mainly inspired by the iconic *sumie* (the old Japanese ink paintings), the overall environment is never terrifying, and mythology and reality blend together to give life to the oneiric travels of the boy who only has a simple human dream: to reunite with his mother.

During the 1970s, Tōei often turned to the staff of other little production companies, which had in many cases been launched in the previous years, such as Tatsunoko Productions (founded in 1964, especially involved in television series[*]) and A Productions (in 1976 renamed Shin'ei Dōga), created in 1965 by Ōtsuka Yasuo and Kusube Daikichirō.

TOKYO OLYMPICS: NEW HEROES AT THE HORIZON

The year 1964 was a decisive year for Japanese economic development. In particular, three concurrent events contributed to pave the way to its future strength: the country became a member of the OECD (Organization for Economic Cooperation and Development); the first *Shinkansen*, the trains connecting Tokyo to Osaka (in that period, the fastest in the world), were inaugurated; and above all, it was the year of the Tokyo Olympics. These were all symbols of the level that Japan had reached in terms of modernity, becoming one of the most promising productive countries and, at the same time, ideally detaching from the Asian context.

---

[*] Production IG (formerly called *IG Tatsunoko*) derived from this company. In 1975, animator Satō Toshihiko from Tatsunoko launched Ashi Productions, and also, Studio Pierrot was founded, thanks to another group of independent artists in 1979.

In particular, every detail of the Olympic Games was planned to give a futuristic aspect to the Japanese archipelago. New technological instruments were introduced, and the games were broadcast by satellite in color. Thanks to the international staff of experts called to train Japanese athletes, Japan won 16 gold, 5 silver and 8 bronze medals, an objective never achieved before.* To underline the quick recovery from the war and the end of occupation, Sakai Yoshinori, an athlete born in Hiroshima on August 6, 1945, was chosen as the torchbearer.

Many shadows pertaining to social and political life were hidden from the general audience and sometimes even banned from television broadcasts[†]: students' protests, criminality, the condition of orphans, among others. A general optimistic image of the country was preferred, and the worlds of manga and animation contributed to the dream, producing many works on sports. Very successful were the comics by Kajiwara Ikki *Star of the Giants* (*Kyojin no hoshi*, 1966–1971) and *Tiger Mask* (*Taigā masuku*, 1969), both adapted into animations, where the heroes—a baseball player and a wrestler, respectively—featured tragic, elegiac and sometimes divine personalities. As in the prewar period, sport was once again a means to glorify the power of the country with its heroes, which could evoke many political, cultural and mythological instances. On one hand, characters such as the orphan protagonist of *Tiger Mask* represented those men who were torn between their sense of *giri* ("social duty") and *ninjō* ("personal feelings"), facing adventures in which their self-sacrifice well matched their personal tragic dimensions. On the other hand, they could also represent nihilistic heroes, such as ninjas, who were considered splinter members of society. These characters had been especially popular from the end of the 1950s in comics: in that period, the

---

* The "Witches of the Orient," Japan's national women's volleyball team who won the gold medal, became a real symbol of the country's fortitude, and at the same time, they influenced the production of many animations dedicated to young girls with magic powers, as we will see in the next chapter.
† For a detailed analysis of television strategies of this period see Chun (2007).

word *gekiga* ("dramatic pictures") was created. According to one of the first cartoonists of this genre, Tatsumi Yoshihiro, *gekiga* were addressed to adults, since they preferred the psychological insight over the characters and their actions were described in a realistic tone, with no comic gags.

Among the most successful authors of these mangas, which were mainly distributed through *kashihon'ya* ("booklenders shops"), Tatsumi preferred gangster atmospheres and Satō Masaaki hard-boiled fiction and thriller mangas. One of the most interesting was Shirato Sanpei (nom de plume of Okamoto Noboru and son of the famous painter Okamoto Tōki), who had also been a *kamishibai* painter and had a very cinematic and action-like style. His debut series was set in the Muromachi period and entitled *Manual of Ninja Arts: Legend of Kagemaru* (*Ninja bugeichō Kagemaru den*, lit. 1959–1962). The leading character Kagemaru is a ninja with a revolutionary spirit, who sides with the rebellious peasants living around the castle of Lord Fushikage. To represent the chaos of this society, battle scenes are bloody and realistic, and they become a symbol of the contemporary protests, especially of students, against the renewal of the U.S.–Japan Security Treaty in 1960.

In the following years, several filmmakers tried to adapt this manga series to animation, but it was only in 1967 that the first movie was presented, made by one of the most important live action directors of contemporary Japanese cinema, Ōshima Nagisa. He had already experimented with an innovative animation in his previous *Yunbogi's Diary* (*Yunbogi no nikki*), completely made by photographs joined through dialectical editing. He used a multiplane stand composing the original images by Shirato through camera movements and quick editing. Keeping the original drawings and the cinematic tools of the manga, the final result retained the original subversive impact, adding an even more subjective perspective of the political fight.

Other works by Shirato were adapted into animations, sometimes losing their original spirit. Among others were the TV series *Fujimaru of the Wind* (*Shōnen ninja kaze no Fujimaru*, 1964–1965), *Sasuke* (1968–1969) and *Kamui the Ninja* (*Ninpû Kamui gaiden*, 1969). *Mangas* with political themes gradually disappeared during the 1970s, and their success was substituted by the elegiac and historical ones.

ALIENS FROM TEZUKA OSAMU'S WORLD

Monsters such as Godzilla, which symbolizes nuclear holocaust, represented not only the wicked effect of science but also the risk that a similar danger was always in ambush and could come again from an "alien" dimension outside Japan. In live cinema, a specific genre was dedicated to this topic, and many of these movies were directed by Godzilla's creator, Honda Ishirō, such as the popular *The Mysterians* (*Chikyū boeigun*, 1957). However, the terrifying elements of this genre, more than being linked to the possible destruction of the country, consisted of the terrifying features of the main characters, usually represented as inhumane and insensitive beings, mechanically walking and fighting like soldiers.

In the immediate postwar period, aliens became popular, also thanks to the comics by Tezuka Osamu (1928–1989), known as the God of manga, who had started his career in 1946 after graduating in medical sciences. In 1947, he was the first to publish a one-volume manga of 200 pages, *New Treasure Island* (*Shin takarajima*, inspired by Stevenson's work*), that clearly revealed him being influenced by European cinema and Disney's and Fleischers' animation. The story, with little dialogue, was mainly narrated by means of visual tools such as multiple planes, angles and even time ellipses and fade outs.

---

* Tezuka had worked with a small group of artists and publishers in Osaka, producing the so-called "red books of manga" (*akahon manga*, printed on cheap paper and often sold in the streets) before moving to Tokyo, where he began publishing some of his most famous works in magazines, including *Kimba the White Lion* (*Janguru taitei*, lit. *Jungle Emperor*, 1950–1954) and *Princess Knight* (*Ribon no kishi*, lit. *Knight of Ribbons*, 1953–1956), later adapted into animated series.

His most internationally acclaimed work was the science fiction manga *Astro Boy* (*Tetsuwan Atomu*, lit. *Mighty Atom*), with twenty-three volumes published between 1952 and 1968.* Set in 2003, it is the story of a little robot with human feelings, made by Dr Tenma with the features of his own dead son. When the scientist realizes the robot will never grow up, he sells it to a circus to be used as an attraction in robot fights. Ransomed by kind professor Ochanomizu and finally brought back to the Department of Sciences where it had been created, Astro Boy will face many adventures, saving the Earth from various dangers, thanks to its special body provided with weapons and its ability to flight.

A hybrid between Pinocchio and Frankenstein, this character is fundamental in the history of Japanese animation for many reasons. It was the first to clearly represent the new kind of warrior, that is, a pure-spirited child who uses a powered exoskeleton, but in a particular way. The scholar Tom Gill has specified the difference between the words *henshin/henkei*, meaning "transformation," and *gattai*, meaning "combine bodies" (Gill, 1998). In the following decades, *gattai* will soon become a widely used expression in the world of animation, often represented by young heroes who fight by means of their mechanical exoskeletons, never biologically transforming. In this case, Astro Boy undergoes a kind of metamorphosis, from a machine to a child, able to have feelings and even suffer, but it is a painful and lonely transformation, coupled with the sadness of having been abandoned by his father. During the occupation, the policy of technological nation-building (*gijutsu rikkoku*) was strongly supported, meant to enhance the industrial modernization of the country. However, in Tezuka's work, little Astro Boy becomes a symbol of innocence and moral integrity, despite the evil effects of adults' corruption, and of those who use machines for negative aims.

---

* It followed a pivotal work of 1952, *Emperor Atom* (*Atomu taishi*), and it was not his first comic on aliens, since he had already published *The Mysterious Underground Men* (*Chiteikoku no kaijin*, 1948), *Metropolis* (*Metoroporisu*, 1949) and *The World to Come* (*Kitarubeki sekai*, 1951). Many others followed.

"Manga is my wife, but anime is my lover," Tezuka asserted years later in an interview.* On January 1, 1963, the God of manga launched the series *Astro Boy* (*Tetsuwan Atom*, based on his own mangas) for Fuji Television, which in autumn of that same year was also broadcast in the United States by NBC.† It was not the first animation produced by Tezuka. After his collaboration with Tōei Dōga, in 1961, he had founded his own production company called Tezuka Osamu Dōga Production—one year later renamed Mushi Productions—where he gathered some of the best animators of that period, including his favorite Sugii Gisaburō.‡

Tezuka's aim was to produce commercial animations to finance other experimental animated movies.§ *Tales of the Street Corner* (*Aru machikado no monogatari*, 1962) was the first of 16 experimental shorts produced between 1962 and 1988. In a narrow street, many characters—a little girl, some mice, a moth, many wall posters, a lamppost and a tree—independent of their being organic or not, merge their feelings in a choral harmony, which is broken only by a war.⁵ This movie, the first to win the prestigious Ōfuji Noburō Award, also represents a kind of research on the expressive potentiality of animation, as the rich visual style of wall posters demonstrates.

In the same year, Tezuka also produced *Male* (*Osu*), a three-minute funny short about a couple of cats in a dark room that are being disturbed by their stressed owner (who has just killed his partner). These first two movies were planned and produced

---

* The interview is found in the movie *Animation Maestro Gisaburō* (id., 2012) by Ishioka Masato. The word *anime* was created by Tezuka himself as a contraction of *animēshon* (animation), from that moment on used to refer to any kind of animation.

† Before *Astro Boy*, other animation series had been produced in Japan, such as *Otogi Manga Calendar* (*Otogi manga karendā*, 1962, 312 educational episodes on historical events). *Astro Boy* was sold in about 20 different countries.

‡ Sugii had already worked with Tezuka, for example, as an animator for *Panda and the Magic Serpent*.

§ Tezuka clearly said he had no interest in television programs made by Mushi: https://www.dailymotion.com/video/xb5zqb.

⁵ War is one of the recurring themes in Tezuka's work.

by Tezuka with the support of his outstanding staff of animators: Yamamoto Eiichi, Sakamoto Yūsaku, Sugii Gisaburō,
Tsukioka Sadao, Rintarō, Yamamoto Shigeru, Tanaka Eiji, Nogi
Yukio and many others.* They also worked on the making of the
Astro Boy television series, produced with a very low budget as
thirty-minute episodes. To lower the costs, they used limited animation, in that period called modern design, which was already
used by American animators. Instead of the usual six frames per
second, Tezuka's staff made it even slower, as one single drawing
could be repeated for eighteen frames by means of techniques such
as *hikiseru* (dragging of the cels during the shooting), the variation of angles and the insertion of lines to simulate movement.

Since *Astro Boy* displays many international features—
characters and settings are not ethnically and culturally defined—
and also thanks to the contemporary success of the animations
dedicated to aliens such as *The Jetsons* by Hanna-Barbera, the
series was very appreciated in America, but NBC stopped broadcasting it after two years, considering some of the contents too
violent for a young audience.† In 1964, Mushi also produced a
feature film for the Japanese Fuji Television entitled *Astro Boy:
Hero of Space* (*Tetsuwan Atomu: Uchū no yūsha‡*), co-directed by
Yamamoto Eiichi, Hayashi Shigeyuki and Takagi Atsushi, a collage of three episodes of the TV series linked together through
unreleased parts.

Mushi's experimental production continued in 1964 with
two shorts: *Memory* and *Mermaid* (*Ningyō*). Through a collage

---

* Some of Mushi's animators launched different production companies. Tezuka him-
self, even before the failure of Mushi in 1972, founded the new Tezuka Productions
in 1968. In the same year, Sugii Gisaburō with other animators launched the Group
TAC; Tanaka Eiji established the Tama Productions in 1970 and the Sotsueisha Group
in 1972 (renamed Sunrise in 1977); Rintarō, Dezaki Osamu, Kawajiri Yoshiaki and
Maruyama Masao founded the Madhouse in 1972.
† Other series by Tezuka were successfully presented in the United States, including
Treasure Island and *Kimba the White Lion*.
‡ It became a practice to link television series episodes for theatrical releases. This is the
case of the feature film *Kimba the White Lion* (*Chōhen janguru taitei*, 1965), which was
awarded the Golden Lion prize at the Venice Children's Film Festival in 1967.

of images and photographs, the first one shows how our experiences of life are differently impressed in our memory, with the risk that a global war may delete all recollection of human beings. *Mermaid* is a minimalist homage to fantasy and individuality, narrated through the dream of a child who finds a fish and imagines it as a mermaid, but he is considered insane and has to give up the illusion.

Four more experimental movies followed in the 1960s. *Cigarettes and Ashes* by Tsukioka Sadao anticipated by 35 years Dreamworks' film *Chicken Run* (2000), being the story of the rebellion of a chicken and the final escalation to war. *Drop* (*Shizuku*, 1965) narrates broken illusions, here represented by a man adrift on the sea who desperately tries to drink the only drops remaining on his raft's mast. *Pictures at an Exhibition* (*Tenrankai no e*, 1966) is featured in ten episodes, each describing with different techniques the various human typologies determining war, power, religion and greed—with the musical accompaniment of the suite by Mussorgsky. *Genesis* (*Sōseiki*, 1968), the last experimental short before a pause of about 20 years, is a parody of John Houston's *The Bible* (1966), narrated through fixed images describing the creation of the world and its inclination to self-destruction.

EXOTIC AND EROTIC

During the second half of the 1960s, the comics industry had reached its full maturity and had clearly defined its various genres for specific audiences, on the whole identifiable in manga for children (*kodomo manga*), for young boys (*shōnen manga*), for young girls (*shōjo manga*), for adult men (*seinen manga*) and for women (*rēdisu manga*—ladies). Also, live cinema and animation had launched many productions tailored for similar targets.

As a consequence of the change of the urban structure—most of the families moved to the periphery of big towns—many movies, especially actions and *pinks* (as the soft-core films were called), were addressed to the leftover audience living in the central areas, mostly made of young and single students and office workers. The binomial sex-violence favored by this audience soon became a successful formula also for comics and animations addressed to adults, starting from the manga series *Lupin III* (*Rupan sansei*) created in 1967 by Monkey Punch (nom de plume of Katō Kazuhiko) and inspired by Maurice Leblanc's *Arsène Lupin*. His adventures were full of action, comic gags and erotic references. In 1969, a short movie based on this manga series was produced as a pilot episode for the television series.[*] Shot in CinemaScope, directed by Ōtsuka Yasuo and co-produced by Tokyo Movie and A Production, many extraordinary animators contributed to the making of this film, including Sugii Gisaburō and Kobayashi Osamu. In particular, Sugii animated the female character, Mine Fujiko, who added a strong erotic nuance to the action of the story.

Sugii, together with Yamamoto Eiichi, Sugino Akio and Dezaki Osamu, was one of the protagonists of the most important erotic production of these years, the trilogy of feature films on the whole known as *Animerama*,[†] produced for Mushi and Nippon Herald by Tezuka Osamu: *A Thousand and One Nights* (*Sen'ya ichiya monogatari*, 1969), *Cleopatra* (1970) and *Belladonna of Sadness* (*Kanashimi no Beradonna*, 1973). The first and longest (130 minutes), directed by Yamamoto Eiichi, tells the adventures of the poor, Aladdin who falls in love with the slave Miriam. Separated due to intrigue, Miriam dies while giving birth to their daughter, and Aladdin leaves to seek his fortune. Years later, when he is the king of Baghdad, he meets and sexually desires a young woman, ignorant of the fact that she is his own daughter. The erotic elements are fundamental, including Sapphic sexual intercourse and incest. However, rather than representing a voyeuristic ploy,

---

[*] The first series was broadcast in 1971, soon followed by feature films, including Miyazaki Hayao's debut movie *Lupin III: The Castle of Cagliostro* (*Rupan sansei: Kariosutoro no shirō*, 1979)—he had already been the author with Takahata Isao of the television series.

[†] Tezuka chose this name to summarize animation, cinerama and drama.

they somehow become instruments of new animated experimentations, especially in the scenes where a few lines fluidly melt bodies with a liquid effect, the use of chiaroscuro in the opening and closing scenes, the live cinema inserts, and the psychedelic rhythm given by the music score.

Cleopatra, co-directed by Tezuka and Yamamoto, is an homage to the arts of every period and culture, celebrated by means of a rich parade—sometimes ironic—of the main icons of world history. Following an experiment, the spirits of three friends are transported from the twenty-first century to the period in which Cleopatra lived in Egypt and reincarnated into different beings. They can follow the sad story of this woman and her unhappy relations with her lovers, until her final desire to die. Like in the previous movie, the staff of animators makes several technical experiments, such as inserting live action scenes into drawings, animating famous paintings of French Impressionism and other artistic currents (for example, a naked Mona Lisa). Some interesting hybrids among cultures are performed, such as the scene where Julius Caesar dies in pure *kabuki* style; however, the most interesting visual aspects of the films are linked to the erotic scenes: in the metamorphosis of bodies during sexual intercourse, the lines become quite rarefied, de-territorializing the senses and almost dissolving their carnality. To Cleopatra, sex becomes a symbol of her solitude, as the lyrics of the song underline: "Nile flows, Cleopatra's tears. It's the desert. Wind blows, Cleopatra's sighs."*

In 1973, the new president of Mushi, Kawabata Eiichi, commissioned to Yamamoto the direction of the last of the *Animerama* trilogy, *Belladonna of Sadness*,† based on *La sorcière* (1862) by Jules Michelet. On the day of her marriage to Jean, the beautiful Jeanne is abducted by the local Lord and raped by his soldiers

---

* The song *Cleopatra's Tears* (*Kureopatora no namida*) is performed by Saori Yuki.
† Sugii Gisaburō was the director of animation. He especially was the author of the main character, *Belladonna*.

as a violent *ius primae noctis*. This is only the beginning of a sad series of events she is the victim of, and for this reason, the devil (represented by a penis shape) approaches her, transforming her into a witch. The story of Jeanne, including her final execution at the stake, represents the destiny of all the women of every period and culture, from the ones who had participated in the French revolution of 1789* to those who fight for gender equality in the contemporary period. Many artistic techniques are employed in this film†: medieval images blended with impressionistic and symbolic paintings, Belladonna's body—continuously exposed to somebody's glance—resembling Aubrey Beardsley's figures, the rough carnality expressed through Egon Schiele's colors and the painful scenes often inspired by Munch's atmospheres. This scenario was interspersed with many peculiar Japanese inserts, not only the background made by the painter Fukai Kumi but also traditional landscapes and Japanese pop art memorabilia.

Unfortunately, this ambitious film was not a success and proved to be insufficient to save Mushi Productions from bankruptcy. It has recently been re-evaluated, thanks to some special screenings in prestigious festivals, including the Toronto J-Film Pow-Wow and Locarno Film Festival, both in 2009.

THE INDEPENDENTS OF PUPPET ANIMATION

MOM Film Studio launched by Mochinaga Tadahito in 1960 collaborated with Videocraft International in the making of some feature films by Rankin-Bass, including *Willy McBean and His Magic Machine* (1965) and *Rudolph the Red-Nosed Reindeer* (1964). In these films' credits, Mochinaga Tad (the name he used) was listed as the supervisor of animation, but in fact, he was the director of all the scenes made in Japan, based on his own scripts and on the

---

* In fact, the film closing scene is the image of *Liberty Leading the People* (1830) by Eugène Delacroix.
† *Belladonna* is mainly made with fixed images made in watercolors, oil paintings and ink drawings, often composed by the overlapping of painted glass plates. Only a few scenes are animated, especially the ones where Jeanne is a victim of violence.

dialogue pre-recorded by the American company (Ono, 1999). At the same time, MOM Film Studio-produced animated television series for the international market, and Mochinaga kept on working with Shanghai Film Production.* Thanks to this pioneer animator, some of the best puppet animators of the next generation could train and learn these techniques. Among them were the two masters-to-be, Kawamoto Kihachirō and Okamoto Tadanari.

Born in Tokyo in 1925, Kawamoto had worked shortly at Tōhō before being fired for a conflict with the unions. For a period, he made dolls by reproducing famous people that were used as images in the magazine *Asahi Graph*. Together with the artist Iizawa Tadasu, he also made puppets to be used in the photographs inserted in to illustrated books.† In the same period, he watched *The Emperor's Nightingale* (*Císařův slavík*, 1949) by Jiří Trnka and was so strongly affected that he decided to become an animator. In 1953, he joined Mochinaga's staff, and in 1958, together with Iizawa, he finally established his own production company, Shiba Productions, where he mostly directed animated commercials. However, Kawamoto felt the need to find a personal style, and for this reason, he contacted Trnka: in 1963, he moved to Prague to study with him for 1 year, before going back to Japan.

In 1968, Kawamoto made his first animated short,‡ *The Breaking of Branches is Forbidden* (*Hanaori*, lit. "Folding Flowers"), the story of a young acolyte of a temple who unsuccessfully tries to protect a cherry tree. This first movie clearly shows the animator's preference for the Japanese traditional theatrical atmosphere and aesthetic. Thanks to the mask-like puppet features, the performing style, the backgrounds, the overall atmosphere and music

---

* In 1981, Mochinaga organized in Tokyo the first retrospective on Chinese animation, selecting the works produced by Shanghai Film Production. In 1985, he was invited for one year to teach animation at the Beijing Film Academy.

† See the interview with Kawamoto at the link: http://www.midnighteye.com/interviews/kihachiro-kawamoto/.

‡ Kawamoto's movies were now screened through the system organized by his friend Okamoto Tadanari, who had launched his Echo Incorporated production company. Together, they distributed their works in small circuits, including schools.

score, this work reminds us of *kabuki* and *nō* dramas, with the addition of a subtle sense of humor.

In 1970, Kawamoto made a short movie by using different techniques (puppets and drawings), entitled *Anthropo-Cynical Farce* (*Kenju giga*, based on a short novel by Yokomitsu Riichi), set in a European dog track fin de siècle: metamorphosis and a particular alternation of lights and shadows are displayed to explain the inconsistency of illusions and the uselessness of human greed. It was then the turn of a new puppet animation in a traditional atmosphere, the fascinating *Demon* (*Oni*, 1972*). Even more than in the previous movie, here the characters are not intended to emulate real human beings, but their quintessence, so as to accentuate the tragic experience of the story.

In 1973, Kawamoto's new movie was a paper cut animation, *The Trip* (*Tabi*), a surreal collage of partially animated scenes inspired by the Prague Spring of 1968. Likewise, surreal and also made in paper cut animation, the following *A Poet's Life* (*Shijin no shōgai*, 1974, based on a short novel by Abe Kōbō†), tells the story of a man living in a semi-industrial society who suffers for having lost his job and his mother, finding relief only in becoming a poet. However, Kawamoto was not satisfied with this technique and decided to go back to puppet animation.

Based on the titular kabuki play, which had inspired Ichikawa Kon's puppet animation, in *Dōjō Temple* (*Dōjōji*, 1976), Kawamoto selected atmospheres, colors and settings typical of the paintings of the Heian period, adding the bunraku puppets performance style. Like the original story, Anchin rejects the young Kiyohime, who revenges his refusal by persecuting him and burning him inside a bell. The visual richness and the narrative fascination of this movie are also equaled by the following *House of Flame*

---

* Based on an old tale from *Anthology of Tales from the Past* (*Konjaku monogatari*, written during the Heian period), it tells of two brothers who are threatend by their mother, transformed into a demon.
† In various interviews, Kawamoto highlighted how this character was also inspired by his own experience at Tōhō.

(*Kataku*, 1979), the story of a young woman torn between two suitors, who decides to destroy herself; however, her suffering does not end with her death.

Together with Kawamoto, his friend Okamoto Tadanari is considered one of the greatest puppet animators in Japan, who, in 1961, started his training at MOM Film Studios. In the course of his career, he experimented with various styles and techniques, starting from his diploma film *Mirrors* (*Kagami*, 1961, co-directed with two colleagues), where he used water-like psychedelic fade outs and extreme angles. In 1964, he launched the independent Echo Incorporated, and from 1965, he began making short animated movies alternatively using puppets, paper, cels and objects of any kind (including garbage). Okamoto received eight Ōfuji Noburō Awards, the highest number ever, and many international awards.

Just like Kawamoto had initially been inspired by Trnka, Okamoto was strongly influenced by Břetislav Pojar, whom he was lucky enough to meet. His first, *The Mysterious Medicine* (*Fushigina kusuri*, 1965: the story of two burglars who try to steal medicine from a scientist's laboratory), is made with wooden puppets similar to those in the Czech animator's *The Midnight Adventure* (*Půlnoční příhoda*, 1960) and won his first Ōfuji Noburō Award. After one year, Okamoto made two new short movies, the musical *Welcome, Aliens* (*Yōkoso uchūjin*) and *The Woodpecker Plan* (*Kitsutsuki keikaku*), and then a fourth one in 1970, *The Flower and the Mole* (*Hana to mogura*), all based on Hoshi Shin'chi's science fiction short novels and made with several different techniques. His overall work was more joyful than Kawamoto's, thanks to the variety of colors, music and the funny puppets and settings, but a certain black humor—later fundamental in his work—was also apparent.

Okamoto's production was intense, spanning from television series* to independent animations. In 1972, he professionally joined

---

* Okamoto worked for many television series: *Series of Songs* (*Uta no shirīzu*, 1968–1970), *Everyone's Songs* (*Minna no uta*, 1975–1986) and *The Series Which Mistreats People* (*Ningen ijime shirīzu*, 1973–1980).

Kawamoto, and together, they launched in Tokyo the first edition of the successful festival Puppet Animeshow, which lasted 8 years. In this first edition, Okamoto also presented his last *The Monkey and the Crab—A Japanese Tale* (*Nihon mukashibanashi—Sarukani*) and *The Tree of Courage* (*Mochimochi no ki*), both displaying Japanese traditional atmospheres and experimenting with particular stylistic effects. One of the best examples of this kind of narrative research is represented by his next work, *Praise Be the Small Ills* (*Nanmu ichibyō sokusai*, 1973). The overall narration is performed in a contemporary key, with the lyrics sung with a guitar accompaniment, while the paper cut animation exalts the atmosphere of the demons of the past, so familiar to the Japanese audience.

Once more in a traditional setting, *Towards the Rainbow* (*Niji ni mukatte*, 1977, based on a short novel by Ōkawa Etsuo), is the tender love story between a girl and a boy, who live in two villages that are in conflict and separated by a river; their love will persuade all the villagers to build a bridge, which would allow them to finally be together. Okamoto accurately researched every detail of the original settings of the past, so as to re-create the magical atmosphere.

Thanks to Kawamoto and Okamoto, puppet stop motion was now one of the most favored kinds of animation in Japan. They were not the only ones, and other production companies specialized in this technique, including the Gakken founded by animator Matsue Jinbo,* and the Kyōdō Eiga, which also produced stop-motion feature films.

---

* Among the other works, in 1965, Matsue had been the author of *The Red Ogre Who Cried* (*Naita akaoni*) based on the short novel by Hamada Hiroshi. Other famous animators specialized at Gakken, including Watanabe Kazuhiko and Watanabe Ryūhei.

CHAPTER 4

How the West Was Won

THE TOKYO OLYMPICS HAD ideally concluded the first phase of reconstruction in Japan, which had started in 1945. A slogan coined by the media, 100 million people in a state of trauma (*ichiokumin sōkyodatsu*), was used to indicate the collective effort made over a period of twenty years to strengthen mass culture and the three basic units of society—job, family and education—from which the new model of bourgeois family was born.* Thanks to the stability of the middle class, during the 1960s, a new slogan, the mass mainstream of 100 million people (*ichiokumin sōchūryū*), replaced the previous one and was intended to indicate the new economic power of the country and the new position of the mass, now at the center of the economic, political and cultural scene (Zunz, 2002). The mainstream middle class was

---

* Basically made of an office worker father distant from his family, a housewife keeping their suburban home clean and sons or daughters competing for entering the best schools and becoming office workers. This model, however, was often negative, as Ueno Chizuko argues: "The Japanese Oedipal triangle in the modern family, therefore, consists of a disappointing father, a frustrated mother and a weak-willed son" (Ueno, 2005).

now able to express specific demands and to deeply influence the supply, both nationally and internationally.

However, in the beginning of the 1970s, the economic dream was partially broken because of two main events: the "Nixon Shock" of 1971 and the 1973 oil crisis.* These caused a rift in the relations with Japan's Western partners; as a consequence, during this decade, the Theory about Japaneseness (*Nihonjinron*)—the authenticity and uniqueness of Japanese culture—was further emphasized. According to this theory, the racial, linguistic and cultural homogeneity of the country is preserved, only slightly shadowed by the ethnic minorities—Ainus, *burakumin* (the Japanese pariah), and immigrants. This ideology reinforced the concept of sociocultural identity, and at the same time, the capitalistic tendency to produce diversified goods was determining the birth of extremely heterogeneous targets. Sometimes called *shōshū* ("micro-mass"), these groups of people wanted to distinguish themselves from the others, and as Marilyn Ivy argues, only a few years later: "Managed mass culture is intimately linked with the rise of the service industries in the 1970s and after. Culture tends to be passively received in the form of 'services' as this systematized, heteronomous production of values becomes normalized within everyday life" (Ivy, 1993).

With the increasing number of specific goods addressed to single targets, many iconic products flooded the market, including those derived from art, animation, and literature. In many cases, they were promoted by special events, where all the fans of the new wonders could meet and experience new identities. The Japan SF Convention (*Nihon SF Taikai*, started in 1962), in the 1978 edition, hosted the first cosplay parade,† which would

---

* The American president decided to intensify relations with China without consulting the Japanese partner and went on an official visit to Beijing on July 15. One month later, Nixon imposed a 10% increase on import duties and soon after devalued the dollar. Also, the oil crisis imposed by the OPEC members shocked the Japanese market, causing the diversification of energy sources, including nuclear.

† The practice to wear manga and animation characters' costumes, in Japanese called *kosupure* ("costume roleplay").

become an annual event from 1980. Through this and other practices of transformation, it became possible to taste for real the experiences of many animated heroes.

MONSTERS ARE ON THE WAY!

The pioneer of Japanese robotics Mori Masahiro has been the first to evaluate the intersections between human and not-human elements in technological applications. In 1970, he published an essay entitled *The Uncanny Valley (Bukimi no tani)*,[*] where he explained how the emotional reaction to robots increases if they look and act like humans, even if their movements are not fluid[†]; however, extreme verisimilitude reveals robots' flaws and causes repulsion.

In the imagery, these concepts are related to android heroes; therefore, the characters use prosthetic exoskeletons, which only partially resemble human beings. The long history of television animated series on androids such as *Iron Man Nr. 28 (Tetsujin 28 go[‡])* began during the 1960s, as we have already seen with *Astro Boy*, and were soon very successful. The genre underwent an evolution during the 1970s, especially thanks to the work by the cartoonist Nagai Gō (nom de plume of Nagai Kiyoshi),[§] in particular from his manga *Mazinger Z (Majingā Z*, published in 1972 and adapted in an animated series in that same year), where Mazinger's mecha-body is controlled by a young boy who sits in the robot's head. There were also some theatrical versions, for example, *Mazinger Z Vs. Devilman (Majingā Z tai Debiruman*, 1973, directed by Katsumata Tomoharu), where the hero and his team

---

[*] Published in Mori (1970).

[†] Many Japanese artists take inspiration from this kind of representation. In particular, Yanobe Kenji uses robots and giant exoskeletons as a symbol of the physiological transformation in the post-nuclear era.

[‡] Based on the 1956 manga by Yokoyama Mitsuteru, broadcast from 1963 and directed by Watanabe Yonehiko and Wakabayashi Tadao.

[§] Nagai had been a pioneer of erotic mangas, including *Shameless School (Harenchi gakuen*, 1972). Almost all his mangas were edited by his own publishing house Dynamic Pro (launched in 1969, later also an animation production company). Many of the television series based on his mangas were produced at Tōei. In the following years, Nagai also invented the transformable robots, starting with the series *Getter Robo* (from 1974).

fight not only against robots but also against demons.* However, this genre was mainly addressed to television broadcast for a very young audience, and little by little, it embedded some iconographic conventions that would strongly contribute to changing the cultural panorama. Recurring elements were the stateless features of the characters and of the architectures of the settings, so as to ideally erase the national borders. Furthermore, the heroes almost always fight as a group, not individually, and each of the members' costumes is characterized by a color that also indicates his or her peculiarities: the leader in red, symbol of victory; the co-protagonist in blue, touchy but equally valorous; the funny character in yellow; the quietest and gentlest one in green; and the troublemaker usually in pink.

In several cases, *kaijū* ("monsters") were markedly a symbol of the negative effects of the Western influence on traditional Japanese culture, thus suggesting that things are often different from what they look like. For example, the catastrophic Tōei movie *Flying Phantom Ship* (*Sora tobu yūreisen*, 1969, by Ikeda Hiroshi)—the story of a young boy who tries to discover who sent a giant robot to destroy his city and learns that it is all part of a plot by the most powerful businessman of his town—suggests that there actually exist many international conspiracies, especially military ones, and that it is necessary to be suspicious of what comes from abroad.†

The television series *Star Blazers* (*Uchū senkan Yamato*, lit. *Space Battleship Yamato*) by Matsumoto Leiji, five times turned into feature films and broadcast from 1974, is different in tone and quality. It suggests a more complex and human image of enemies—identical to the terrestrials they fight in outer space—provided with morals and vulnerable like any human being. An in-depth analysis of these kinds of characters and a more

---

* Devilman had already been the leading character of the titular series directed by Nagai at Tōei, broadcast from 1972 to 1973.
† This film was the first Japanese animation officially distributed in the Soviet Union, in spite of the xenophobia of its plot.

detailed description of technology are displayed in the series *Mobile Suit Gundam* (*Kidō senshi Gandamu*, broadcast from 1978, by Tomino Yoshiyuki*), the first of many animations produced at Sunrise with the label *Gundam*. The fighting cyborgs—characters whose master was the cartoonist Ishinomori Shōtarō†—became an alternative to the heroes in flesh and blood and almost became the protagonists of this genre during the 1980s and 1990s, especially in the home video market.

Among the movies based on television series, one of the best results is represented by the first adaptation of Matsumoto Leiji's *Galaxy Express 999* (*Ginga tesudō 999*, 1977), directed at Tōei in 1979 by Rintarō with the supervision and script by Ichikawa Kon. The young orphan Tetsurō travels on board a flying train throughout the galaxy (a symbol for his passage from childhood to maturity), seeking revenge for the murder of his mother and to find a mechanical body for himself. The mysterious daughter of the evil queen of Andromeda, Maetel, travels with him and they feel a kind of attraction to each other.‡

All these movies were popular enough that they stimulated a huge production of toys reproducing the main characters, which contributed to further spread of their success.

HORROR FROM MYTHOLOGY AND FROM THE WEST

Yōkai ("monsters and supernatural entities") were popular in the animation produced in these same years. Their common trait was the extravagance of forms and powers, and their primary mission was, of course, to disturb the peaceful everyday life of Japanese people!

---

* Tomino was also the author of the series *Neo-Human Casshan* (*Shinzō ningen Kyashān*, broadcast from 1973), among the first animations featuring cyborgs mate at Tatsunoko, which soon specialized in this genre.
† Among his most famous works, the manga series *Cyborg 009* published in 1964 and inspired many movies and television series.
‡ Many successful movies followed and soon other heroes created by Matsumoto were added, including Captain Harlock, later leading to other popular movies.

Generally defined as *shinrei mono eiga* (films on phantoms and on supernatural), the movies where *yūrei* ("ghosts") appeared, which had been produced in the previous decades, were often based on folk tales, with some Western elements; those dedicated to *obake mono* (stories of *obake*, "transforming beings") also contain scenes of mutation, in many cases suggesting human fragility. During the 1960s, *yōkais* were protagonists of the successful television series *Gegege no Kitarō*—whose leading character is a baby *yōkai*, who helps humans to live with other supernatural creatures—many times adapted into movies.[*]

As we have seen, demons (*oni* or *akuma*) like *Devilman* are also often protagonists of animations. Between the 1960s and the 1980s, horror characters deriving from Western tales increased in number, such as *kyūketsuki*[†] ("vampires"). These creatures were similar to the indigenous leech-bat Yasha, considered the reincarnation of death and a revengeful woman, or to the *bakeneko* ("phantom cat"), which at night transforms itself into a woman to suck men's blood—all terrifying elements because of their combination of blood and death, both considered as impure by Shintoism.

A funny television series—a mix of live action and animation—was produced by Tezuka Osamu, with the title *Vampires* (*Banpaiya*, broadcast from 1968), whose leading character was a wolf.[‡] The genre became more popular during the 1980s, especially due to the movies based on the novels by Kikuchi Hideyuki. However, many of these films, although successful, did not reach a high-quality standard, as in *Vampire Hunter D* (1985, by Ashida Toyoo), a hash of science fiction, pornography and gore effects. Sometimes,

---

[*] Born as a manga series that had appeared in 1959, by Mizuki Shigeru, entitled *Kitarō of the Graveyard* (*Hakaba no Kitarō*), this story has often been adapted into movies at Tōei. It is important to remember that Mizuki was also the author of many stories set during the war.

[†] The first Western vampire had been introduced in Japan by the mystery and thriller novelist Edogawa Ranpo with his short novel *Vampire* (*Kyūketsuki*, 1930) and soon blended with traditional Japanese elements.

[‡] In the first episode, it is explained that the word vampire is intended for any person who can transform itself into an animal.

they even blended together vampires with *yōkais*, gangster movie inspiration and classical horror atmospheres, such as the noir and gore films directed at Madhouse by Kawajiri Yoshiaki (for example, *Wicked City—Yōjū toshi*, 1987).

Also, mummies and zombies had been imported into Japan in recent times, and they achieved the greatest popularity during the 1990s. As for Frankenstein's monster, it acquires a peculiar meaning in Japan, since its creation involves the manipulation of organs.* The anthropologist Margaret Lock has underlined how in Japan organ transplant is a social rather than a clinical matter (Lock, 2002): as the dichotomy between the definitions brain-dead corpse (*nōshitai*) and brain-dead person (*nōshi no hito*) suggests, a person might still be alive while his organs are cannibalized for donation. Animation has often interpreted the sense of panic deriving from organ transplant and genetic engineering. The most interesting examples are once again works produced by Tezuka Osamu's team. Based on the cartoonist's own manga *Dororo* (*Dororo to Hyakkimaru—Dororo and Hyakkimaru*, published from 1967), the team headed by Sugii Gisaburō made an excellent television series, which was broadcast for the first time in 1967 by Fuji TV.† In the Tokugawa period, before a decisive battle, a lord barters his victory with forty-eight demons by promising the organs of the son who is going to be born. The child survives but is abandoned on the flow of a river. Then, he is rescued by a medicine man, who transplants the missing artificial limbs. Trained as a warrior, he will fight against the demons to reclaim his own organs. The action scenes, the demons' iconography and the theme of abandoned children belong to the Japanese tradition‡; in addition, the Frankenstein-like assembly of his organs and

---

* There are of course some animations based on Mary Shelley's work, such as *Mystery! Frankenstein Legend of Terror* (*Kyōfu densetsu kaibutsu: Furankeshutain*, 1981, by Serikawa Yūgo).
† There is also a live-action version directed in 2007 by filmmaker Shiota Akihiko.
‡ A child abandoned to the waters in Japan is also linked to the idea of an altered motherhood. The word *mizuko* (an "aborted fetus"), literally means "child of the water" and is also related to *jizō*, the bodhisattva, who protects the never-born children.

the idea of a kind of Pinocchio who is looking for his real body suggest that human beings need their integrity to distinguish themselves from monsters. Moreover, the series also has as subtext Tezuka's concern about the alchemist-like intervention on the body, which may eventually become a symbol of the brutality of science. He would often introduce this theme in later works. For example, when the Japanese government approved gene recombination experiments in 1984, he produced and codirected with Okuma Kimiharu the feature film *Bagi, the Monster of Mighty Nature* (*Daishizen no majū Bagi*, 1984), the story of a half-feline and a half-human chimera—its name Bagi is inspired by Disney's Bagheera (from *The Jungle Book*)—who is the product of a genetic engineering experiment* and befriends a young boy.

In analyzing the horror movies, which openly present the fear that science and technology are used in a harmful and evil way, one cannot exclude the animations produced in the 1970s and 1980s describing the nuclear tragedies of Hiroshima and Nagasaki. Among the most interesting ones, an experimental short of 1978, *Pikadon* (ibid.,† which received an award at Annecy in 1979), by the independent filmmaker Kinoshita Renzō,‡ summarizes in only seven minutes the terrifying explosion of August 4, 1945, on Hiroshima. Apart from the explosion itself, the main horror elements consist of the scenes when all people look toward the sky, and a flash transforms the images into monochrome signs of

---

* Years later, a similar character appeared in Takada Yūzō's manga and its animated versions, *Cat Girl Nuku Nuku* (*Bannō bunka neko musume*, 1997), where a cat's brain is transplanted into a gynoid's body.
† The word refers to two onomatopoeia: *pika* means "something shining" and *don* the "roar's sound".
‡ Produced while employed as a publicist, he also worked as an animator at Mushi for both the series of *Astro Boy* and *Cleopatra*. With his wife Sayoko, he founded the Studio Lotus, where he produced the internationally acclaimed *Made in Japan* (1972, Grand Prix winner at the New York Animation Festival). When the city of Hiroshima was selected by Asifa (*Association Internationale du Film d'Animation*) as the location of the new Hiroshima International Animation Festival (*Hiroshima Kokusai Animēshon Fesutibaru*), Kinoshita and his wife were the organizers and inaugurated it in 1985. Sayoko has been the director of the festival since the death of Kinoshita in 1995.

death. Even if the final scene opens to the hope for a better future, Kinoshita's movie is intended to shock the audience, showing how reality may be more frightening than fiction.

Both live cinema and animation have adapted the manga series *Barefoot Gen* (*Hadashi no Gen*, 1973–1974), written by Nakazawa Keiji, a cartoonist from Hiroshima who had lost his family and had been a victim of radiation himself. The first animated and titular feature film*—which won the Ōfuji Noburō Award—was directed in 1983 by Mori Masaki and produced by Gen Productions and Madhouse. It tells the story of little Gen and his family during the explosion, emphasizing in the first part of the movie how hard life was before it. Like in *Pikadon* by Kinoshita, a dazzling light makes everything monochrome and silent. Together with the tragedy of the thousands of casualties, fire burns everything to ashes and a black rain falls, contaminating the survivors.

During the 1980s, many other animations describing post-nuclear settings were produced for both television and cinema, such as *Fist of the North Star* (*Hokuto no Ken†*) and *Future Boy Conan* (*Mirai shōnen Konan*, directed by Miyazaki in 1978).

EPIC, MYSTERY, MAGIC AND EROTICISM: HEROINES BEYOND ROMANTICISM

The word *shōjo* ("young girl") has a clear assonance with *shojo* ("virgin") and in many animations, the two terms suggest the erotic substrate of the stories. The so-called *Shōjo Culture* (*shōjo bunka‡*) includes *mangas*, animations and even music: it

---

* Based on different mangas dating back to 1986 by the same author, a new adaptation—not as good as the previous one—was made in 1986 by Hirata Toshio, entitled *Barefoot Gen 2*, telling what happened to Gen 3 years after the end of the war.
† Protagonist of mangas and television series, and of a feature film produced by Tōei in 1986, directed by Ashida Toyoo.
‡ *Shōjo Culture* was born in the Meiji period, but its success was achieved mainly in the post-war period, also thanks to the *dōjinshi* (magazines, mangas and novels by amateurs, sometimes with erotic nuances), and reached the peak of success starting in the 1980s.

always describes a no man's land suspended between childhood and maturity, where sexuality is still partially encrypted. The stage troupe Takarazuka, exclusively composed of women who also perform the male roles, owes its success to the same kind of sexual stylized ambiguity, something that the female audience is particularly fond of.

Images reproducing *shōjos* (called *jojōga*) in the beginning of the twentieth century used an abstracted depiction of women, mainly with thin bodies and big eyes. In the 1950s, it changed to resemble more the French doll iconography, such as Tezuka Osamu's *Princess Knight manga* series he had modeled on Takarazuka's artists: eyes with a spark to show emotions, a big head compared to the body, and long arms and legs. The stories of the young heroines became richer in psychological descriptions and with their dialogue, and the settings were no longer of the traditional Japanese background.

Many cartoonists during the 1960s were women, such as the "Queen of manga" Takahashi Rumiko and some authors belonging to the Year 24 Group (*24 nen gumi**), including Ikeda Riyoko of the famous manga of 1972, *The Rose of Versailles* (*Berusaiyu no bara*). They all added narrative richness to the plots by means of various themes, not only romantic but also science fiction, political and epic. Moreover, they often used ambiguously sexualized male characters known as *bishōnen* ("beautiful young boy", particularly loved by women readers), and as a consequence, many stories called *shōnen ai*† ("love between boys") about homosexual love became very popular.

Bishōjo hīrō ("beautiful heroines") were often represented as brave warriors, without losing their female (and sometimes

---

* The name derives from the year of their birth in the Shōwa era, that is, 1949. At the end of the 1980s, another all-female group of cartoonists called CLAMP debuted with even more mature themes—often adapted into animations—which also were followed by the male audience.
† Also called Boy's Love (BL), they are mainly romantic stories, with the most erotic ones also called *yaoi* ("*Yama nashi, Ochi nashi, Imi nashi,*" "no climax, no denouement, no meaning"). The feminine equivalent are called *yuri* ("lily") or Girl's Love.

markedly erotic) characteristics—such as the ninja protagonist of *Wrath of the Ninja* (*Yōtōden*, 1989) by Yamasaki Osamu—and even gynoids in science fiction movies were shaped with sinuous bodies.* More interestingly, in these years, a new kind of heroine gained increasing popularity, partially inspired by the Witches of the Orient—Japan's national women's volleyball team, winner of the gold medal at the Tokyo Olympics of 1964, which for many years was considered as a symbol. Parts of these productions were related to the supernatural and magic sphere: the vampire woman, among others, is a recurrent character in animations such as *Vampire Princess Miyu* (*Kyūketsuki hime Miyu*†). Linked to the idea that women have a peculiar nature, heroines with extrasensory powers also became common, such as *Mai the Psychic Girl* (based on the 1985 manga by Kudō Kazuya). However, the biggest success was achieved by the stories related to young girls endowed with *mahō shōjo* ("magic powers"), often a symbol of the new social power achieved by women, as the ironic series of animations based on Takahashi Rumiko's popular mangas *Urusei Yatsura* (published from 1978‡) and later the most popular Takeuchi Naoto's mangas *Sailor Moon* (*Bishōjo senshi Sērā Mūn*, published from 1991) demonstrate. This latter example, in particular,§ the story of a fourteen-year-old girl and her team whose magical powers are activated by means of a brooch, is the portrait of a normal teenage world—young girls

---

* An exception is represented by *Dr. Slump* (a television series and some feature animated movies based on the 1980 manga by Toriyama Akira), where the little gynoid Arale looks like a small and ugly girl.

† A gothic retelling of the myth of Dracula in the body of a thirteen-year-old girl, who is destined to never grow up. Based on an original story by Hirano Toshiki and Kakinouchi Narumi, adapted in 1988 in four features for home video, a TV series and a manga version.

‡ The word *urusei* has the double meaning of "annoying" and the star Uru, while *yatsura* means guys. The leading character Lum is the daughter of a demon who faces many adventures and at the same time lives as a normal high school girl. Many animated adaptations originate from this manga: a successful television series directed by Oshii Mamoru and various features films, including the first two *Urusei Yatsura: Only You* (1983) and *Urusei Yatsura 2: Beautiful Dreamer* (1984) by Oshii himself.

§ The first feature film, *Sailor Moon R The Movie* (*Gekijōban Bishōjo senshi Sērā Mūn*), was directed in 1993 by Ikuhara Kunihiko.

who dream of getting married, fall in love and cry. All this blends with violence and eroticism (including platonic homoerotic relations); furthermore, their innocence is represented by their school uniforms,* which barely cover their bodies during the fights. As a matter of fact, after the *Animerama* trilogy, many other erotic animations had been produced from the 1970s, including *Yasuji's Pornorama: Do It!* (*Yasuji no porunorama—Yacchimae!*, 1971, from a manga by Tanioka Yasuji). The birth of the home video market—especially thanks to the private viewings of movies—facilitated the spread of these productions, sometimes blending erotism and soft-core pornography, paving the way to a new genre called *hentai* ("pervert"), still very popular today,† which we will refer to in the next chapter. Many subgenres also originated, such as erotic-horror‡—*Urotsukidōji—Legend of the Overfiend* (*Chōjin densetsu Urotsukidōji*, 1987, by Takayama Hideki), establishes a precedent for excessive animations often adapted from the mangas by Maeda Toshio.

THE INDEPENDENTS, AN ALTERNATIVE TO THE MAINSTREAM

Since the 1960s, independent filmmakers have increasingly produced personal works. Among the names already mentioned, Kuri Yōji has always been one of the more active, often winning prestigious international awards. His surreal short movies continuously examined the aberrations of human beings—people who consider sex, food and money as the only values of their existence—narrated with extreme images: violence, metamorphosis, physiological functions and strange creatures born from corpses—as

---

* The schoolgirl-Lolita image is also linked to the business of the shops of *burusera* ("bloomers" and "sailor," that is, their uniforms), where it is also possible to buy young girls' underwear for fetishistic purposes.

† The first *hentai* animation was *Lolita Anime* (1984), a blend of extreme sexual perversions—including pedophilia and incest—followed by *Cream Lemon* (1984, first episode of a long series).

‡ This movie was also the first of the so-called tentacular porno, where, most often, young girls are raped by monsters with enormous tentacles.

in *The Midnight Parasites* (*Kiseichō no ichiyoru*, 1972, which received an award at Oberhausen in 1973).* Still very active as a painter, since his debut, he has represented independent animation in the world. Many retrospectives have been dedicated to his work—including the one at the Museum of Modern Art in Paris in 1988—and he has also been awarded with the prestigious Asifa Prize at Annecy in 1993. Among his last animations, in 2006, he took part in the Image Forum Tōkyō Loop project (a collection of independent shorts by different filmmakers) with his grotesque-comic *Rolling Excrements* (*Funkorogashi*).

Among the animators who had debuted at Sōgetsu, many continued to work in different fields, such as Wada Makoto, who only occasionally directed animations. His *Murder!* (*Satsujin*, 1964, winner of the Ōfuji Noburō Award) was an astonishing parade of styles and references to cinema and literature, but he alternated live action movies† with his career as a novelist, translator, illustrator and musician—this latter interest also inspired his animation *Zigomar The Mysterious Thief: Musical Version* (*Kaitō Jigomā—Ongakuhen*, 1987, based on an original story by Terayama Shūji).

Tanaami Keiichi‡ is one of the most famous Japanese pop artists, but he is also an illustrator, cartoonist, video artist and animator. Most of his work is related to his war trauma, especially of the bombing on Tokyo, which he had witnessed when he was a child.§ After his debut animation *Marionettes in Masks* (*Kamen no marionettotachi*, 1965), he traveled to the United States, where he met Andy Warhol and other artists. American culture later became an inspiration for his own works, and in fact, his first

---

* Among the other recurrent themes, one is the inertia present in people's lives, in *Pop* (1974), another is the empty rituals of human passion, illustrated in the comic sketches of *Manga* (1977).

† Wada has been particularly awarded for his two live actions *Mah-jong Hōrōki* (*Mājan hōrōki*, 1984, lit. *Vagrancy Book of a Mah-jong Player*, from a novel by Asada Tetsuya) and *Uneasy Encounters* (*Kowagaru hitobito*, 1994).

‡ A complete profile of this artist is available at: http://www.ubu.com/film/tanaami.html.

§ Tanaami also refers to this matter in his recent works, such as *A Gaze in Summer* (*Natsu no shinsen*, 2002).

animations after his return were experimental shorts inspired by his icons: *Goodbye Elvis Presley and USA* (*Sayōnara Erubisu Puresuri USA*, 1971), *Goodbye Marilyn* (*Sayōnara Maririn*, 1971), and *Oh Yoko!* (1973). In all of them, Americans' obsessions with music, sex, drug, cult leaders, unidentified flying objects (UFOs) and popular singers and actors are displayed. In 1975, Tanaami made some of his best animations, including the autobiographical *Sweet Friday* (*Yasashii kin'yōbi*), *The Bride Stripped Bare by Her Bachelors* (*Kanojo no dokushin monotachi ni yotte*, on the sexual obsession of the Japanese for Lolitas) and *Crayon Angel* (1975, about his memory of the war). In 1981, he was on the threshold between life and death because of a very serious illness, an experience that later influenced his work. Many famous artists such as Murakami Takashi have declared to have been inspired by the work of this master—who also gets credit for having launched new talents such as Tabaimo. His abstract images full of meaning still gift the audience an adrenaline-filled vision of space, time and memory, such as in the music video *Diamond Sleep* (2013) from the *Red Road* album by the group Haunted Leather.

Starting in 2000, Tanaami worked for years with the filmmaker Aihara Nobuhiro,* producing about a dozen works before Aihara's death in 2011. For this author, memory and the unstoppable flowing of time were recurring themes, especially referencing his childhood experience near an American military base. He had debuted as an animator with *Rain* (*Ame*) in 1968, while working at the small Studio Zero Production founded by cartoonists Ishinomori Shotarō and Fujiko Fujio, together with the experimental animator Suzuki Shin'ichi. He made about 80 films (from 2008 in video format) while collaborating with other minor studios—all abstract and lyrical, alternating drawings and photographs, circular forms and mandalas, and extreme metamorphoses. Human beings are only reduced to simple signs

---

* They were both academics at the University of Art and Design of Kyoto.

or to their external shape, empty like the trail that remains of their existence in the memory—such as in *Poisonous Snake* (*Yamakagashi*, 1972): a young girl with no face waits outside her home while her mother prostitutes herself with American soldiers. After traveling around Europe for a period, his works became even more oneiric, deepening his experimentation with space (such as in *Stone*, 1975, made in Sweden). To his growing interest in movement, lights and their effects on bodies—particularly in *Image–Shadow* (*Eizō–Kage*, 1987) and *Mask* (1991)—he added research on Buddhist nuances of sound, silence, the "non-visible," for example, in the short *Wind* (*Kaze*, 2000).

REALITY FROM DIFFERENT PERSPECTIVES: HARADA HIROSHI AND KUROSAKA KEITA

Harada Hiroshi, inspired by Terayama Shūji and Winsor McCay, made his first animation *The Weak Dinosaur* (*Jiyowana kyōryūchan*, 1976), when he was only fourteen years old. In 1978, his new *Retaliation at Dawn* (*Akatsuki no hōfuku*) won an award at the Fuji Concours, and one year later, he won another prize at the Japanese Festival of Image (Nihon Eizō Fesutibaru) with *Reward at Dawn* (*Akatsuki no hōshū*), starting his relentless career. His graduation work at the Academy of Design of Tokyo, *The Death Lullaby* (*Nidoto mezamenu komori uta*, 1985), was awarded with the first prize at the Pia Film Festival*: it tells of the bullying of a young boy against a background of events—including the protests against the construction of Narita international airport—which had deeply changed Japanese society. Harada's style is deliberately shocking and distressing; he deforms buildings and roads, subverts perspective, and interchanges violent lights with blood surfaces and live scenes: his particular style accounts for him having been accused of using subliminal messages.

---

* Prestigious experimental film festival launched in 1977, linked to the titular film magazine.

Harada started working for various television series, while at the same time continuing his own independent works. He decided to make an animation based on the controversial erotic-grotesque manga *The Camellia Girl* (*Shōjo tsubaki*, 1984) by Maruo Suehiro, which was a free adaptation of a *kamishibai* piece, but given its violent contents, he did not manage to find a production company that would support this project and had to produce it himself with the help of some underground circuits. The musician J.A. Caesar, author of the music scores of Terayama Shūji's works—from which many scenes of the film derived inspiration—also agreed to work with him. After five years, the movie was ready, entitled *Midori* (*Chika gentō gekiga - Shōjo tsubaki*, lit. *Underground Projected Dramatic Pictures: The Camellia Girl*, 1992). Set at the end of the nineteenth century, it is the story of a young orphan girl who joins a circus where malformed people work, and they mistreat, rape and enslave her, until an illusionist dwarf takes her as his own lover and protects her. The movie was censored for its scenes of sex, violence, torture on animals and discrimination against disabled people, but for the filmmaker, these were necessary for the *mise en abîme* of a kind of Theater of Cruelty. As Harada himself claimed, he was interested in love stories among imperfect people and also in a counter-history of Japan, showing the true exercise of power by governments and the suppression of people. His work has since then continued along the pipeline of mainstream and independent animation, theatrical performances and video art, always distinguishing itself for the peculiar style and the approach to human beings.

Likewise eclectic, Kurosaka Keita is one of the main independent animators of the last decades,[*] ranging from video art to animation and music videos. After his graduation from the Musashino Art University in 1979, Kurosaka spent 2 years in Paris,

---

[*] It is necessary to mention at least some of the contemporary eclectic artists: Iimura Tadahiko, Yamamoto Shigeru, Fukushima Shinji, Ōi Fumio, Sugimoto Gorō, Suzuki Shin'ichi, Yokoyama Ryūichi, Hayashi Seiichi and Itō Takashi.

studying painting with Jacques Yankel. When he returned to Japan, he studied cinema at the Image Forum, trying to define a technique that could best fit his own expressive needs. According to him, animation has ambiguous nuances: "I don't really think of myself as an animation artist. I originally got my start in the contemporary art world. I was always trying to come up with a way of injecting the dimension of time into my work…My biggest problem as an artist was finding a form of artistic expression that would have the same effect as music, but in the realm of painting—the impact of sharing the same time space and physical space among a large number of people. That just happened to turn out to be video, and in terms of specific technique within that framework, animation, but for me animation has never been anything but an extension of my painting work."[*]

In his works, Kurosaka uses different techniques—traditional animation and cut paper, collage and photography—to explore contemporary society and its violence. His first work consists of a group of five shorts made between 1982 and 1986, *Metamorphose Works* (*Henkei sakuhin*), by which he investigated human beings' nature with its contradictions and, at the same time, the origin of art. To Kurosaka, human nature is unstable, because it is conditioned by the flow of time, the mobility of space and the exercise of power. He describes it through continuous grotesque metamorphoses to reinforce the idea that everything is an illusion, such as in the shorts *Sea Roars* (*Umi no uta*, 1988) and *Worm Story* (*Mimizu monogatari*, 1989). His following films—*Personal City* (*Kojintoshi*, 1990), *Box Age* (1992) and *Phonograph Nr. 13* (*Chikuonki 13 go*, 1993)—which mainly describe contemporary society and urban living, received awards in Japan and abroad and were appreciated by critics and audiences alike. With *The Morning Papa Flew* (*Papa ga tonda asa*, 1997, produced for MTV, and winner of an award at Annecy), Kurosaka's inspiration even seems to resemble Kafka's *The Metamorphosis* in the story of a great number of fathers literally flying over Tokyo, and

---

[*] Interview by Ettinger (2010).

analogously in the hyperviolent animation he made for the music video of *Agitated Screams of Maggots* by Dir En Grey (2006*), a *tourbillon* of transformations of a larva-demon abused by a young girl, which becomes a fascinating and grotesque homage to the illusions in human existence.

Together with his academic activity and while making these shorts, for 13 years, Kurosaka had been working on his first feature film, presented in 2010: *Midori-ko*, made with over 20,000 colored pencil drawings. Set in a dystopian Tokyo of the twenty-first century, it is the story of a dream food called Midori-ko, created by scientists to solve the world famine, but it does not want to be eaten and flies away. Fantastic characters and transformations contribute to create a sensual, terrifying and fascinating visual travel through human existence, where the prime principle is "eat or be eaten." A nightmarish atmosphere reminds one of Kurosaka's favorite animator Jan Švankmajer, together with his chiaroscuro effects that bring into mind the masterpieces by Hieronymus Bosch and Francisco Goya.

YAMAMURA KŌJI, THE MAGICIAN OF FORM

Yamamura Kōji's career shares many characteristics with Kurosaka Keita's: they both teach in prestigious universities,[†] work privately in independent studios, are assisted in animation by their wives, and, above all, conceive animation as the most precious opportunity to explore imagination. Yamamura Kōji still prefers manual drawing edited by digital tools, intense work that gives his animation a visual richness rarely equaled. A very eclectic author, he is also an illustrator of books for children and directs music videos, commercials and much more. His filmography can be divided into three groups: the first animations made in the 1980s, representing a playground for experimentation; the

---

[*] Kurosaka also directed a new animated music video for the song *Rinkaku* (2012) by the same band.

[†] Yamamura Kōji at Tōkyō Geijutsu and Kurosaka at Musashino Art, both in Tokyo.

second period dating back to the 1990s, during which he produced many commercial projects, including animations for children; and the last and more mature phase started in the beginning of the new century, with a production mainly addressed to adults. Yamamura Kōji began experimenting with animation when he was only thirteen years old, while at the same time training as a cartoonist.

While he was working on his personal animations and studying at Tōkyō Zōkei University, from 1983 to 1987, he also worked with some studios producing 3D special effects and images for the sets of various filmmakers.* During the same period, he developed a passion for the works by Ishu Patel, Jurij Norštejn, Priit Pärn, Okamoto Tadanari and Mochinaga Tadahito, by whom he would later be inspired.† The 16mm short diploma film *Aquatic* (*Suisei*, 1987), made with modeling clay on backlit glass slabs, already shows his preference for fluid images, which are continuously and softly transformed into something different.

Between 1987 and 1989, he worked at Mukuo Studio, while at the same time becoming a member of the group Animation 80‡ and producing his independent movies. Among these, the multi-awarded *Japanese-English Pictionary* (*Hyakka zukan*, 1989) was made with different techniques (clay, puppets, photographies, drawings on cels and live images) to compose—again in a rapid mutation of shapes—a kind of pictorial encyclopedia of animation technique.§ *Looking for Things in the Box—The Search of the Researcher* (*Ochikochihō no hako—Hakase no sagashi mono*, known as *Perspektivenbox*, 1990), again made with different techniques, including 3D, shows modern and capitalistic cities excessively crowded with buildings, objects, animals and people in paroxysmal images.

---

* Including for the remake of *The Burmese Harp* (*Biruma no tategoto*, 1985) by Ichikawa Kon.
† From http://www.yamamura-animation.jp.
‡ This group, to which also Kurosaka Keita belonged, was mainly formed by young students who periodically used to organize screenings of their own works.
§ http://www.yamamura-animation.jp/e-filmo.html#s.

In 1993, Yamamura Kōji and his wife Sanae, a painter, launched the production company Yamamura Animation, where he started directing clay animations for NHK TV, targeted for children—including the story of the little birds *Karō and Piyobupt* (*Karō to Piyobuputo*, 1993), *Mr. Kipling* (1995), *Pakushi* (1995) and *Kid's Castle* (1995). The last short made for NHK, *Bavel's Book* (*Baberu no hon*, 1996, based on the work by Jorge Luis Borges), anticipated the style of his future production: a boy and his sister at a bus stop find a book containing a Tower of Babel, from which they are swallowed up into wonderful adventures, described with different techniques and by means of an extremely rich film grammar.

In 2002, Yamamura Kōji's most ambitious short—it had taken six years to be completed—was ready: *Mt. Head* (*Atamayama*), an adaptation in contemporary Tokyo of the titular *rakugo* theater piece. Its drawings, with colors recalling the best of Paul Klee's works, tell the story of a solitary and stingy man who eats some cherry seeds. As a consequence, a cherry plant grows on his head, and his troubles become even worse when people gather around it. A caustic portrayal of the Japanese middle class narrated by means of a traditional song performed with a shamisen background, this short film obtained international success, numerous prizes and even an Academy Award nomination in 2003.

Since then, Yamamura Kōji's career has been even more intense. Among the many short films made from 2003 up to now, all very personal experiments on movement and imagination, is the touching *The Old Crocodile* (*Toshi o totta wani*, 2005), from the titular short novel by Léopold Chauveau. It tells the story of a crocodile that suffers from rheumatism and is no longer able to catch its own food. The delicate *A Child's Metaphysics* (*Kodomo no keijijōgaku*, 2007) consists of a series of surreal sketches on the secret world of children. *Franz Kafka's A Country Doctor* (*Kafuka inaka isha*, 2007), co-produced with Shōchiku and the recipient of an award—among other prizes—at the Ottawa Festival, is a Western-set story coupled with the narration by actors of *kyōgen*. It represents the oneiric and visionary mental flow by distorted images meant to magnify human senses, while fear and insanity are suggested by the various eyes sprinkling in the snow. *Muybridge's Strings* (*Maiburijji no ito*, 2011), co-produced with the National Film Board of Canada and NHK TV, focuses on the idea that the photographer's 24 cameras had somehow captured time, which becomes the leitmotiv of the story: the time corresponding to the real life of this man and, simultaneously, time linking humanity and its history. *Five Fire Fish* (2013), made by means of the McLaren's Workshop application for iPad produced by the Canadian National Film Board, represents one of the many experiments made by Yamamura Kōji.

Among his most recent titles, *"Parade" de Satie* (*Sati no paraado*, 2016) bases its written quotes and surreal images on both the ballet *Parade* that the pianist Erik Satie composed in 1916 with Jean Cocteau and Pablo Picasso and on the life of Erik Satie himself. Thanks to the ballet theme and to the fundamental music score,* Yamamura Kōji's images rapidly evolve to show a continuous flow of different signifiers. The latest film by Yamamura Kōji is *Notes on Monstropedia* (*Kaibutsu gakushō*, 2016), a particular pictorial book on monsters inspired by the European medieval imagery, each moving and acting according to a particular sentence and concept—i.e. "Taste of Tears." Distant from any conventional film grammar, here more than ever, camera movements are rarefied, images have no depth, and narrative develops from the fascinating, meaningless juxtaposition between phrases and almost static characters. Animation thus becomes the freest of the arts.

TEZUKA OSAMU'S LAST EXPERIMENTS

During the 1970s, the "God of manga" had mainly worked on his cartoons. He went back to animation in 1978[†] with *One-Million Year Trip: Bander Book* (*Hyakuman nen chikyū no tabi—Bandā*

---

* Performed by Willem Breuker Kollektief.
† In the same year, he became the director of the Japan Animation Association (*Nihon Animēshon Kyōkai*, known as JAA), a role that after his death passed on to Kawamoto Kihachirō.

bukku, co-directed by Sakaguchi Hisashi), the first of a series of movies co-produced until 1986 with other majors, mainly for television broadcasting. They all told the audience about his consideration of human beings, nature, and the aberrations of science and politics: *in vitro* fertilization of children raised by robots (*Phoenix 2772: Love's Cosmozone—Hi no tori 2772—Ai no kosumozōn*, 1980, directed by Sugiyama Suguru); the fear of a new war (among others, *Brema 4—Angels in Hell—Buremen 4—Jigoku no tenshitachi*, 1981) and, even worse, of a nuclear war (*Fūmoon—Fūmūn*, 1980, directed by Tezuka); pollution and the need of ecological intervention (again *Fūmoon*, but also *Unico*, 1981, by Hirata Toshio); and spirituality in any form (such as in the Shinto-Buddhist substratum of *Phoenix 2772: Love's Cosmozone*[*]).

During the making of these movies,[†] Tezuka once again started the production of his experimental short films. The first was *Jumping* (1984), inspired by the whole shot, seen through the eyes of a child, of an insect during its flight in the Hungarian *The Fly* (*A légy*, 1980) by Ferenc Rofusz. It uses a unique sequence shot: a girl jumps higher and higher, crossing lands, towns, and a war and falling in the underworld, before going back to the initial location. Full of ironic gags, the short is composed of a wide variety of angles and perspectives and uses an essential design with simple colors for the backdrops. In this way, the focus is entirely on the movement, the true protagonist of this experiment.

One year later, it is the turn of *Broken Down Film* (*Onboro firumu*, 1985), set in the Far West, where a cowboy and a woman

---

[*] In 1984, the Italian Rai TV commissioned Tezuka to produce a television series based on the Bible. The series was completed by Dezaki Osamu after the director's death, in 1992, and entitled *In the Beginning: The Bible Stories* (*Tezuka Osamu no kyūyaku seisho monogatari*).

[†] Starting from 1978, the Japanese NTV broadcast a kind of telethon entitled *Love Saves the Earth* (*Ai wa chikyū o suku*), for which the Tezuka Production made some animations, including the ones listed here and *Undersea Super Train: Marine Express* (*Kaitei chōtokkyū Marine Express*, 1979).

have a relationship interrupted by a bad man and a series of abnormalities of the film (noises, lines, misfire and breaks of the visual trace, all typical defects of an old film). The funniest moments are in the scenes where the hero fights both his enemy and the technical problems caused by the bad preservation condition of the film, for example, by climbing from one frame to the other.

In 1987, Tezuka made three new short animations: *Push (Osu)*, *Muromasa* (id.) and *Legend of the Forest (Mori no densetsu)*. The first one consists of brief caustic sketches in which the author resumes and accentuates his anxiety about the fate of Earth, destined to an encroaching but inevitable decline due to the blind development of technology. *Muromasa* is the name of a sword stuck in a straw puppet (*wara ningyō*, used by antiquity for whack curses). A samurai finds it, and from that moment on, he is obsessed with the idea of having to break any straw puppet he encounters, just to realize each time that he has actually killed a person. The message of peace and nonviolence, though very strong, is in this animation more bitter than in the previous titles, to the point of omitting the usual irony that distinguishes Tezuka's work. *Legend of the Forest* is an incomplete work,* as only the first and fourth movements dedicated to the Symphony No. 4 by Tchaikovsky have been completed. The first movement tells the story of a flying squirrel and of his sad destiny tied to the cruelty of a woodcutter who deprives him of his family and later of his partner. The whole story unfolds through different techniques that follow the evolution of the animation itself: the first images are paintings that turn within a zoetrope, then drawings in Émile Cohl's style and later in more advanced animation techniques, including Disney's and Fleischers' and the technique of limited animation. The fourth movement is related to a similar theme: a ruthless team of woodcutters headed by a Hitler-like man is about to deforest an area

---

* Tezuka Makoto, son of the author and also a filmmaker (known as Tezka Macoto), has many times announced that he would continue his father's animation, with no results up until now.

where animals, fairies and gnomes live. Their cruelty is punished by nature itself through a magical plant that grows up to swallow men and machinery, covering them with flowers. As in the famous Disney's *Fantasia*, there is no dialogue but an exhaustive mimic grammar contributes to the development of the story.

The last experimental film by Tezuka is the very short *Self-Portrait* (*Jigazō*, 1988, about 15 seconds), made as part of a collective project. One year before, US artist David Ehrlich, a member of Asifa, had started to gather nineteen short movies by some of the members of the association from five different countries, including the Japanese Kinoshita Renzō, Kawamoto Kihachirō and Tezuka Osamu. The result was the movie *Animated Self Portraits* presented at Annecy in 1989. Tezuka chose to divide the images into three areas reminiscent of a slot machine (whose noise is also the only background sound), alternating in each band a different appearance and combining the different solutions in three handle pulls, until, at the fourth attempt, he composes his own caricature, from whose mouth comes the jackpot. Many different interpretations have been given for this short: that the randomness of the slot machine would indicate the alternate fortunes of his career or that this could represent his last divertissement. In fact, Tezuka died by stomach cancer on February 9, 1989, when he was only sixty years old, in the same year as Emperor Hirohito's death*—both marking the end of an era.

---

* The Emperor's funeral raised various controversies due to the Shinto ritual, which offered a still partially divine image of Hirohito: two symbolic divinities had thus died.

CHAPTER 5

Simulacra

O N APRIL 15, 1983, the Tokyo Disneyland theme park was inaugurated, the first non-American one and a pioneer of a long series of similar Japanese entertainment venues born in the 1980s leisure boom (*rejā bumu*). Unlike what had been imported so far, the new center of attractions had a different nuance of values than the American model, though it represented a faithful iconographic reproduction of the original. As a place suspended between reality and fantasy, for Japanese people it represented a kind of global culture shaped by the contribution of local imagery, tamed by native aesthetics. The carnival of symbols mainly derived from the United States was now blended with local media productions, paradoxically marking a cultural independence from the West.

The park's inauguration took place in the midst of the bubble economy, contributing to strengthening the widespread nationalistic sentiment that accompanied the frequent economic successes of the Japanese archipelago. In addition, Tokyo Disneyland immediately received broad favor not only among children but also among young adults. The young adults were generally indicated by the word—partially negative—*shinjinrui* ("new race"), as opposed to the *kyūjinrui* ("oldest"), or baby boomers of the post-war period.

They were mostly born during the 1960s, had not experienced any of the post-war difficulties, and had been enjoying the increasing social welfare. They were considered people with no traditional values and with few social responsibilities. Compared with the previous generations, they had received a better education but were more conservative, less willing to socialize, more nihilistic and at the same time more individualistic. Another difference lies in the evident contrast with the pacifist ideal of the 1970s, as the post-war generation tended to magnify violence through various media (in particular manga and animation) within the solitude of the domestic walls. The expanding home video market, especially the Original Video Animation (OVA*) which included the extreme erotic and pornographic *hentai*, contributed to feeding their world, as well as the many iconic comics and magazines, beginning with the prestigious *Animage* edited by the publisher Tokuma since 1978, protagonist of the growing phenomenon of anime fandom.†

For a few *shinjinrui*, the border between reality and fantasy soon became feeble, leading them to ideally identify themselves with successful heroes such as Gundam, with the violent harassers of the young Lolita figures of various *hentais*, or in some cases to develop a pathological form of solipsism. This is the tragic case of the serial killer Miyazaki Tsutomu, a fetishist obsessed with erotic anime and pornography, who abducted, raped, killed and cannibalized four little girls between 1988 and 1989, recording his acts with a video camera. When he was arrested, nearly 6000

---

* Original Video Animation refers to animated films directly produced for the video market. The first title, *Dallos*, was produced by Studio Pierrot in 1983 and directed by Oshii Mamoru. The equivalents for live cinema are V-cinema (Video Cinema) or simply Original Video (OV). Both markets have undergone an inevitable decline with the spread of digital and on-demand videos, but there is now a clear resumption of production intended for the web.

† *Animage*'s pages offered the works of some of the most beloved artists, including Miyazaki Hayao, who here published his work *Nausicaä of the Valley of the Wind* (*Kaze no tani no Naushikā*) between 1982 and 1993. Other similar magazines were *Animec*, *My Anime* and *Animation Magazine*.

videotapes were found in his home, predominantly of violent and erotic subjects. The definition of *otaku* was applied to him, a term that literally means "his home" and that would later serve to denigrate the perverse self-marginalization of individuals who are subject to alienation, amplified by manga and animation.

However, in these years, many of the dreams were still set in faraway worlds, often belonging to glorious periods of ancient cultures, a trend that had been established in the previous decade and that, for some time, still represented a successful formula of animation.

THE ENCHANTED WORLD OF MIYAZAWA KENJI

In the 1970s, several television series were co-produced with European studios,* often based on the old world's literature for children. One of the most famous is the adaptation by Takahata Isao (with Miyazaki Hayao's drawings) of the novel *Heidi* by Johanna Spyri, entitled *Heidi, Girl of the Alps (Arupusu no shōjo Haidī)*, whose incredible success stimulated the production of similar products. In particular, Nippon Animation launched the production of various television series labeled as *World Masterpiece Theatre (Sekai meisaku gekijō)*, broadcast from 1975 until the early 1990s, and in 1986, it inaugurated the series *Animated Classics of Japanese Literature (Seishun anime zenshū)*, consisting of the adaptation of famous novels of native literature.† As it often happens, many episodes were later reassembled to produce feature films, while other subjects were directly adapted into films, such as *I Am a Cat (Wagahai wa neko de aru*, 1982, by Natsume Sōseki), directed by Rintarō, or even the ambitious and successful adaptation of the ninth-century classic *The Tale of Genji (Genji monogatari*, by Murasaki Shikibu), directed by Sugii Gisaburō in 1987.

---

* Among the most notable, in 1974, the series dedicated to the well-known Italian *Calimero* was started, directed by Serikawa Yūgo.
† In 1976, the Group Tac launched the series *Japanese Folklore Tales (Manga Nihon mukashi banashi)*.

Among the various titles, some of the most popular are based on Miyazawa Kenji's works,* one of the most beloved authors of children's literature. In 1949, Tanaka Yoshitsugu had adapted into animation his short novel *Gōshu the Cellist* (*Sero hiki no Gōshu*, also known as *Gorsch the Cellist*), followed by a remake in 1963 by the puppet animator Matsue Jinbo and in 1982 by Takahata Isao in a titular feature film awarded with the Ōfuji Noburō Award. Set in the early years of the Shōwa period, it is the story of a young cellist who learns to play his instrument, as well as learning dedication, perseverance, passion and rigor, thanks to the help of some animals. Takahata's version required six years of work to produce the richness of plans, the complex variation of movements, and the fidelity of the animation rhythm to the musical base. The result is a poetic tribute to youth and to the strength of talent, a small gem in the filmography of this filmmaker, which anticipated his mature period at Studio Ghibli, which would start only a few years later.

Among the best adaptations from Miyazawa's works, two were directed by Sugii Gisaburō: *Night on the Galactic Railroad* (*Ginga tetsudō no yoru*, 1985) and *The Life of Budori Guskō* (*Guskō Budori no denki*, 2012). The first title, awarded the Ōfuji Noburō Award, adapted the same tale that had already inspired Matsumoto Leiji for his manga series *Galaxy Express 999* (*Ginga tetsudō 999*, published in 1977, which would later become the inspiration for an animation series). It tells of young Giovanni's journey on a mysterious train—only at the end he will discover that all other passengers are dead—directed to an unknown place of the Milky Way, representing a metaphor for the inner growth of the protagonist, as well as a spiritual voyage to explore the tragedy of death and pain resulting from the loss of the people we love.

With the exception of three humans, the characters are anthropomorphic cats, despite the fact that felines in Miyazawa's works often represent negative beings. In the film as well as in

---

* 1896–1933, he was a poet and author of children's literature.

the original work, the train's interdimensional movement in space and time symbolizes the two moments of the country's main economic and political growth: the period contemporary to Miyazawa, when Western and Eastern elements were blended together,* following the Meiji Positivism, and the economic boom of the 1980s, before the bubble burst.

Similar feelings fill *The Life of Budori Guskō*, once again interpreted by anthropomorphic cats. Young Guskō loses his family because of cold and drought and takes a trip in search of his place in the world, finally finding a job at the volcanic station of Ihatov. This film also portrays the lead character at the center of a drama of death and disillusion, once again revealing the possibility of building a positive future. During the film's production, on March 11, 2011, the Tōhoku area where the story was set was hit by a violent earthquake and a tsunami, resulting in the nuclear tragedy of Fukushima; in the light of this recent event, Guskō Budori's fate was more dramatically perceived.

MASTERS IN THE WORLD OF PUPPET ANIMATION

In the 1980s and 1990s, the pioneer of stop-motion animation Mochinaga Tadahito continued his brilliant mission as ambassador of both Japanese and Chinese animation, thanks to his close collaboration with the Hiroshima Film Festival and the Shanghai Animation Studio. He directed his last film in 1992, *The Boy and the Little Raccoon* (*Shōnen to kotanuki*), and died in 1999 at the age of 80 years.

Okamoto Tadanari also prematurely died in 1990. His latest works, as usual made by means of different techniques and animation styles, represent further examples of his genius and eclecticism. *The Buckwheat Flowers of Ogre Mountain* (*Onigakureyama no soba no hana*, 1979), for example, represented an experiment

---

* Among the many symbols of cultural hybridism, this included the choice of giving two Italian names (Giovanni and Campanella) to the protagonists, the use of Esperanto and Japanese in the titles and the European setting of the village mixed with Japanese elements.

in combining cels and water colors, obtained by painting other colors on a thin layer of plaster laid on the base, so as to recreate the ancient Chinese and Japanese atmosphere of landscapes. For *The Magic Ballad* (*Okonjōruri*, 1982, the tale of the special friendship between an old woman and a magic fox that can cure illnesses with music), he used *hariko* ("paperback puppets") and *doro ningyō* ("terracotta dolls") for the first time, with some sequences made with ink drawings.

Okamoto's last film, one of his masterpieces, unfortunately was unfinished at the time of his death, and was then completed by his friend Kawamato Kihachirō. *The Restaurant of Many Orders* (*Chūmon no ōi ryōriten*, presented in 1991) was the adaptation of a short novel by Miyazawa Kenji, telling a very simple story: two hunters in a forest reach a strange restaurant, where they learn what being prey means. Rich images made by means of acrylic gouache on cels alternately describe warm and wicked atmospheres, and the use of the multi-plane stand helps make uniform the chromaticity of the set and give depth to details. This short was awarded several prizes, including the Ōfuji Noburō's Prize, the eighth to Okamoto, unfortunately posthumous.

Kawamoto Kihachirō died in 2010, at the age of 85 years, but continued to work relentlessly until 2006. Even when not directly involved in film direction, he was an important contributor to puppet animation, as in the NHK TV dramas *Historical Doll Spectacular* (*Ningyō rekishi supekutakuru*), *Romance of the Three Kingdoms* (*Sangokushi*, 1982–1984) and *The Story of Heike* (*Heike monogatari*, 1993–1994), for which he created hundreds of puppets and coordinated the animation teams. In 1981, Kawamoto made his first feature film, *Ren'nyo and His Mother* (*Ren'nyo to haha*), devoted to one of the most influential figures in the history of Buddhism.[*]

---

[*] The screenplay was written by the live-action filmmaker Shindō Kaneto, author of works with mystical atmospheres such as *Onibaba* (1964).

After a few years spent making puppets, Kawamoto returned to directing in 1988 with the ironic *Self Portrait* for David Ehrlich's project and with the film *To Shoot Without Shooting* (*Fusha no sha*, based on *Meijinden* by Nakajima Atsushi), co-produced by the Shanghai Animation Film Studio. It tells the story of Chinese archer Ji Chang, who is longing to become the best archer in the world, and of his long, tiring self-edification that will eventually allow him to hit his targets without using the bow. The film thus becomes a parable about how to overcome ambitions for a higher idealism, a dimension similar to *satori*, while no longer contaminated by desire.

After many years, Kawamoto went back to Jiří Trnka's studio, the deceased animator who had inspired his early works, and directed the short film *Briar Rose or The Sleeping Beauty* (*Ibara hime mata wa Nemuri hime*, 1990). The Czech team actively worked with the Japanese staff to realize this work, and the puppets are stylistically hybrids between the two cultures.* Among the misty atmospheres of an old European castle, the plot is a variation of the fairy tale of Sleeping Beauty: the princess discovers that when her mother was young, she had fallen in love with a man, later believing that he had been killed in war. Now thirsty for vengeance for having been betrayed by her mother, the man is only placated when the princess sexually offers herself to him. Kawamoto is especially interested in the sexual and psychological maturation of the princess,[†] narrated with elements of drama, disenchantment and a bit of cynicism.

After a short film of 1996 (*Rihaku*), Kawamoto succeeded in involving thirty-five different animators from different countries[‡]

---

* One of the gems of this film was that the puppet that was used for the queen's husband was similar to Jiri Trnka himself.

† The narrator is skillfully voiced by actress Kishida Kyōko, also the protagonist of *Woman of the Dunes* by Teshigahara.

‡ Among the animators, in addition to Kawamoto, were Jurij Norštejn, Raoul Servais, Shimamura Tatsuo, Kuri Yōji, Aleksandr Petrov, Břetislav Pojar, Co Hoedeman, Takahata Isao, Mark Baker, Jacques Drouin, Yusaki Fusako, Kurosaka Keita, Yamamura Kōji and many other emerging young authors.

in an experimental project entitled *Winter Days* (*Fuyu no hi*, 2003): using the ancient practice of collaborative poetry (*renga*, consisting of several poets compiling a verse from the last line of the previous one), each director was asked to add a short animation as a poetic stanza, starting with the verses of poet Matsuo Bashō. This project points out the many possibilities offered by animation in terms of techniques, styles and poetics, despite the extreme brevity of each contribution, but above all, it becomes a precious journey into the world of animation.

In 2005, Kawamoto completed his second feature film, *The Book of the Dead* (*Shisha no sho*, from the titular novel by Origuchi Shinobu), which premiered at the Karlovy Vary Film Festival in the Czech Republic. Set in the Nara period, when Buddhism was introduced into Japan from China, it tells of the noble Iratsume—again with the voice of Kishida Kyōko—and of her attraction toward the new religion and the image of Buddha. One day, ignoring the ban on access to women, she imprudently enters a temple and discovers that the image she was worshipping actually belonged to the wandering spirit of a man condemned to death. Thus, the film suggests many themes: human suffering and oppression, spiritual relief and charity, illusion and the possibility of disenchanting from earthly things and the woman's passage to adulthood.

In addition to the works of these masters and among the artists who had professionally grown in the same years, one needs to remember the clay animations by Magari Fumiko and Fusaki Yusako. Magari Fumiko had trained at the MOM Film Studios with Mochinaga, collaborating with the animations for Rankin-Bass and later for some of Okamoto's titles. Like many of her colleagues, her commitment had been more commercial (especially for commercials) in the 1970s, but at the same time, and in particular with her independent Magari Office (Magari Jimusho), she made several short films, mainly for children, using puppets as animated toys, with a delicate and personal style (among others is the short *The Little Bear Oof—Kuma no ko Ūfu*, 1983).

A colorful and dynamic childhood world, enriched by a continuous stream of metamorphosis is the characteristic of Yusaki Fusako's work, an artist who has been living in Italy since 1964, where she initially produced television commercials. Her animations, all made with plasticine, are liquid transformations of shapes, a perfect harmony of motion and fleeting images that mesmerize while they quickly evolve into something else. Yusaki Fusako has been the author of many television series, mostly broadcast by the Italian Rai and the Japanese NHK and Fuji TV. Alternatively, she has made shorts to experiment with the variations of colors, numbers and shapes. Her experimentalism has given birth to many masterpieces, including her shorts of the late 1970s and early 1980s like the delightful *The Ballad of the Tired Man* (*La ballata dell'omino stanco*, 1973), a fascinating dreamlike journey through human existence, and the delicate and poetic *The Wind Rose* (*La Rosa dei Venti*, 2006). One cannot forget that her name is in the group of artists who contributed to the famous *Winter Days* by Kawamoto.

POST-APOCALYPTIC VISIONS

Many essays have been written on the different perception that the Japanese have of the apocalypse, surely different from the awareness of the West. In general, one of the reasons for this difference has been identified in the vector of historical and temporal development, a linear flow in our cultures and a circular flow in some Asian countries. In Japan, this especially refers to the Buddhist concept of *mappō*, indicating the third and last period in history, when a degeneration of moral laws takes place*: a period of rebirth and reconstruction follows, recalling the concrete and recurrent apocalyptic succession related to nature—earthquakes, tsunamis, volcanic eruptions and fires—always followed by new eras.

In 1985, Oshii Mamoru, after the success achieved by the first title for an OVA with *Dallos*, presented his first work made with a personal aesthetic. *Angel's Egg* (*Tenshi no tamago*) opens with the

---

* The three ages follow Buddha's death.

most apocalyptic atmosphere, through a red sky that leaves no hope for humanity. The only characters are a young girl (the angel who protects an egg) and a man who has a crucifix-like weapon with him. Humanity is reduced to statues that remind us of a past existence or to anonymous fishermen who hunt the shadows of cetaceans in the air. Enriched by a surreal visual symbolism, with remarkable homages to Salvador Dalì and Giorgio De Chirico (also thanks to the contribution of illustrator Amano Yoshitaka), the film presents some of the recurring characteristics of his future works: a city in ruin, elaborate war machinery, references to the Bible and native mythology and characters who try to define their own identity.

Angel's Egg, Miyazaki's *Nausicaä* and some other movies from the same year not only suggested the birth of new cultural perspectives, but they also inspired them. The next step in chronological order was represented by *Akira* (1988), Ōtomo Katsuhiro's masterpiece and perfect synthesis of contemporary arts including cyberpunk narrative, based on the manga series by the same author published for the first time in 1982 in *Young Magazine*. The story is set in the capital, renamed Neo Tokyo. As in the movie *Blade Runner* (1982) directed by Ridley Scott, the story takes place in the future, in the year 2019: the city is being reconstructed after the devastation of the planet caused in 1988 by the Third World War, but it is in a state of chaos due to delinquency, factional wars and the attacks of anti-government terrorist movements. A group of scientists study the powers of Akira, a messianic creature who supposedly caused the destruction. Tetsuo, a tragic anti-hero figure and a member of a motorcycle gang, is subjected to new Akira replication experiments. The young delinquents are inspired by the *bōsōzoku* rebels of the 1960s, as terrorist movements recall the failure of student demonstrations and the terrorist attacks by the Red Army of the same turbulent period.[*] However, the dystopian

---

[*] *Bōsōzoku* ("violent racing groups") have existed since the 1950s and are bands of motorcyclists who engage in vandalism, representing one of the most important recruitment sources in the *yakuza* world. The Red Army was a communist and anti-imperialist group founded by Fusako Shigenobu, advocating revolution during the 1970s.

epic of this film extends into a deliberately vague space without a historical background, suggesting themes such as the youth crisis in contemporary society, the disillusionment toward the values of tradition, the cult of power, the corruption of institutions and the aberrant domain of technology.*

The cult of power—here represented by gang competitions, paranormal clashes and government experiments—is at the center of another topical issue of those years: the proliferation of religious sects. The New Religions (*Shinkō Shūkyō*) had developed at the end of the nineteenth century as a syncretic result of Western influences on native religion. A second wave followed in the 1970s as part of the New Age movement, known as "New Religions" (*Shin Shinkō Shūkyō*). One of the most popular sects was the Aum Shinrikyō, founded by Asahara Shōko. It was a blend of religions and philosophies, including the idea that the world was governed by economic powers. The guru also used manga and animation, as well as various foreign sci-fi novels (especially those of Isaac Asimov) to spread his theories and recruit new adepts. Believing in a future risk of apocalyptic destruction, he decided to rebel by putting into effect a massive terrorist attack. On March 20, 1995, five members of the sect deposited bags containing sarin gas in some of the central points of the metropolitan stations in the center of Tokyo, causing 12 deaths and sickening thousands of people, fostering a new wave of demonization of media (especially manga and animation) from which Asahara had taken inspiration.

The attack and its scientific threat stimulated the spread of the syncretic and apocalyptic vision that had inspired Asahara himself: the twenty-six episodes of the television series *Neon Genesis Evangelion* (*Shin Seiki Evangerion*) directed by Anno Hideaki, starting from 1995, gained an incredible success.

---

* Ōtomo had already directed a short on the dictatorship of technology in 1987, entitled *Construction Cancellation Order* (*Kōji chūshi meirei*) in the omnibus movie *Neo Tokyo: Manie Manie* (*Meikyū monogatari*); the other two episodes of the omnibus are *Labyrinth * Labyrinths* by Rintarō and *The Man Who Runs* (*Hashiru otoko*) by Kawajiri Yoshiaki.

The complex plot,* also adapted in feature films,† tells of a world almost totally destroyed by a cataclysm. The apocalyptic symbols of both the films and the series are amplified by a rich Jewish–Christian religious texture, and details on war and technology serve to consolidate the idea of a biomechanical transformation of human beings.

In the same year as the Aum attack, the strongest earthquake registered in Japan since 1923 caused thousands of deaths in the Kobe area: the combination of the two tragedies added to a mix of elements that were already deeply changing Japanese culture. A fundamental factor was represented by the drastic increase of divorces: the fracture in the traditional family institution inspired the creation of young orphan characters in many animations and was also linked to some of the crucial social issues of the period, such as the phenomenon of *hikikomori* (people who withdraw from social life, isolating themselves in their homes), *freeters* (people who constantly opt for part-time employment) and NEET (not in education, employment or training). The invention of the internet was certainly another important factor even if the widespread diffusion in the Japanese archipelago would only be registered in the new century. In 1992, Kobe was chosen as the location for the iNet venue of the Internet Society, an event that gave rise to a growing number of considerations on the use of the new media, which on the one hand was seen as a form of digital democracy and on the other hand was feared because its effects on society were still unknown. Finally, an important factor was the intensification of robotic projects aimed at simulating the human figure, especially in the world of the arts, including

---

* Within the neo-metropolis built to protect people from alien attacks, the Nerv organization uses combat machines, called Evangelions, to defeat the monsters, called Angels, who are threatening the Earth.

† Various titles, including *Neon Genesis Evangelion: Death and Rebirth* (*Shin seiki Evangerion gekijōban—Shi to shinsei*) and *The End of Evangelion* (*Evangerion gekijōban: Magokoro o kimi ni*), both directed by Anno in 1997. The saga also includes several manga volumes, video games, and a new movie tetralogy distributed from 2006 to 2012.

gynoids with a particular techno-sexuality such as the cyborg futuristic pin-ups by the artist Sorayama Hajime.

In the wake of these novelties, the idea of apocalypse came to represent any form of contrast between the individual and what is not rationally perceived or humanly experienced. Once again, at the center of the drama is the idea of metamorphosis and biomechanical contamination, such as in the best animated films dedicated to this field: *Ghost in the Shell—Mobile Armored Riot Police* (*Ghost in the Shell—Kōkaku kidōtai*, 1995, followed in 2004 by *Ghost in the Shell—Innocence,* both by Oshii Mamoru) and *Metropolis* (2001, by Rintarō). The first one is set in 2029 in a fantastic Japanese metropolis: architecturally structured as a vast and wireless web network, the inhabitants are permeated by elaborate cybernetic systems and differ from robots only because they possess a spirit, the ghost, within the shell, the mechanical body. Kusanagi Motoko, head of a governmental section charged with abolishing cybercrime, investigates the Puppet Master, a complex computer program able to transform people's conscience and memory. Bodies become the synthetic casing of their human spirits, indicating the psychic and physiological mutation to which men are potentially subjected.

Metropolis, based on Tezuka Osamu's 1949 manga and only partially inspired by Fritz Lang's film of 1927, is the story of an investigator and his nephew Ken'ichi, who go to Metropolis to hunt for a criminal scientist. They discover a conspiracy organized by the powerful Red Duke, who has also created the little gynoid Tima—a machine that conceals a scientific error, since it is endowed with feelings.[†] Metropolis is the true protagonist of the

---

* Like *Evangelion*, *Ghost in the Shell* consists of a complex multimedia production that includes, in addition to the manga by Masamune Shirō (Shirow), video games, a new film in 2006 entitled *Ghost in the Shell: S. A. C. Solid State Society* directed by Kamiyama Kenji and an American version directed by Rupert Sanders in 2017.
† The friendship between a human being and a gynoid is the theme of other animations, including the successful *Planetarian: Man of the Stars* (*Planetarian: Hoshi no Hito*, 2016, by Tsuda Naokatsu), based on a visual novel.

film, a symbol of the dominance of the inorganic over the living, as demonstrated by its lower level, where the poorest people live together with the enslaved robots.

From the late 1990s, the concept of *sekaikei* ("kind of worlds"*) was used to analyze Japanese subcultures, a neologism in many cases referred to as post-Evangelion syndrome, applied to animations, mangas, video games and light novels.† In particular, it refers to heterosexual love stories between two young people in the background of an apocalyptic scenery, where the protagonists, through their actions, are able to heavily influence the destiny of humanity. Another characteristic is the total lack of institutions and of the reasons for the catastrophe. Shinkai Makoto's film *Voices of a Distant Star* (*Hoshi no koe*, 2002) is considered one of the most interesting examples of *sekaikei*. Mikako and Noboru are great friends, but in 2047, the girl, now a member of the United Nations Space Army, is forced to leave the Earth, keeping in touch with Noboru through messages that arrive more and more slowly. Shinkai explores in detail and with great sensibility the emotions of the two characters, leaving every historical and social contingency in the background.

FAKE DOLLS, FAKE GIRLS: TECHNO-SEXUALITY AND POST-GENDER

Ghost in the Shell—Innocence by Oshii Mamoru was only partially a sequel of the 1995 movie. Set in an unspecified multiethnic city in 2032, detectives Batō and Togusa investigate a series of murders committed by Hadaly 2052 gynoids, sophisticated robots produced by Locus Solus‡—equipped with the spirits

---

* The term was already in use since the 1980s, mainly referring to science fiction (Azuma, 2009).
† It is a rapidly expanding literary genre aimed at young people, usually light volumes illustrated by popular cartoonists.
‡ The name Locus Solus comes from Raymond Roussel's 1914 novel. However, the creation of female fetish bodies has long been a reality in Japan: for example, the Actroid DER2 developed by the University of Osaka and produced by Sanrio's Kokoro Ltd and realistic gynoids coated with simulated silicone skin.

of real girls (who are kidnapped for this purpose)—to serve as prostitutes. Iconically inspired by Hans Bellmer's surreal photographs (Monnet, 2010) and by the pubescent girls of the works by Yoshida Ryō, together with a probable reference to the gilded eyes of children portrayed by Nara Yoshitomo,* Oshii had defined a model of doll-gynoids that did not resemble the common aesthetic of *kawaii* ("cute," "delicate"†).

Rather, the moral implications linked to the adolescent world, in particular the idea that innocence is destined to vanish in adulthood due to social responsibility, find in its dolls-gynoids a greater adherence to the aesthetic of *moe* born at the end of the 1990s: the verb *moeru* means "sprouting", but with different characters also means burning, with a distinct appeal to the traditional aesthetics of fragility and impermanence of what is beautiful and uncontaminated, especially in representing young, innocent and pretty girls. According to Azuma Hiroki, *moe* generates an imaginary feeling, pure and perverse, but at the same time schizophrenic, separating man from the real emotional world (Galbraith, 2009).

Gynoids, in particular, are creatures of a post-gender world (Haraway, 1991). Their replication in *Innocence* is linked to the etymology of the Japanese term *ningyō* ("doll"): the two ideograms literally mean human form, hence a duplicable image, artificial and alterable. There are of course many dissenting opinions, for example, the idea that these gynoids could represent carnality tamed by a cage; the references to Pygmalion and the myth of the beloved statue that finally animates; and repulsion, with regards to a kind of necrophilia fetishism. A similar attitude can be found in the very young Lolitas of many *hentai* productions—in which school uniforms act as an erotic exoskeleton over individuality—in

---

* Photographer Yoshida Ryō is famous for his depictions of dolls, even dissected. Pop artist Nara Yoshitomo's works often portray children with accusatory eyes that denounce violence and their loss of innocence.

† A *kawaii* body is small and delicate, with pastel and tender colors. The same ideal identifies the cases of *roricon* ("Lolita complex"), which forces many men to be attracted by very young girls.

the extremely realistic erotic dolls (also called Dutch Wives*) and in the voluntary transformation of the body through the many styles of street fashion,† cosplay, tattoo and piercing practices.

Over the last twenty years, artists have interpreted this new culture through unusual styles, often iconographically linked to mangas and animations.‡ The most important reference is offered by the indigenous and western elements made superficial (without perspective, meaning hierarchy) in the postmodernist *Superflat* style of Murakami Takashi. He is an author strongly inspired by Japanese animation who also contributed his artistic direction to the small gems *Superflat Monogram* (2003) and *Superflat First Love* (2009). Both are directed by Hosoda Mamoru and dedicated to the collaboration between Murakami and Louis Vuitton. However, it is a culture rooted in the past, especially in the ancient *shunga* erotic prints of the Edo period,§ with their exaggerated representation of genitals, body fluids and erotic abnormalities. *Shunga*-inspired, among others, is the successful animation *The Sensualist* (*Kōshoku ichidai otoko*, 1991, lit. *Life of a Libertine*), adapted by Abe Yukio from the same-named seventeenth century novel by Ihara Saikaku. It is the story of the loving encounters of the most sexually active man in the history of Japan (3742 women and 725 men throughout his life, according to the story), described through a very detailed range of erotic effects fully derived from Edo's artistic culture.

The erotic sphere in extreme animations, including *hentais*, often retains the ability to evoke without revealing, that is, to extract

---

* Dutch Wives feed another subculture online, fueled by the so-called iDollators enthusiasts.
† The Gothic Lolita, Ganguro and Visual Key styles are among the many that have animated Tokyo's Harajuku district for years. Some of these, in particular Visual Key (an expression derived from a band of the 1980s), allow a nearly total metamorphosis of the body for an androgynous effect.
‡ The robotic sculptures by which Yanobe Kenji evokes the fear of a post-nuclear physiological transformation, and the mix between carnality and hi-tech by the artists Bome and Mori Mariko.
§ From the same period, also the bloody images of the atrocious prints (*muzan'e*) that would later influence authors of the erotic-grotesque genre such as Maruo Suehiro.

experiences from a realistic context, so that they can be adapted to each spectator's own perception. The high level of abstraction allows homogeneous fruition by male and female audiences alike, mainly thanks to the emphasis on some androgynous hybrid characters. In some cases, hybridization is particularly acute, for example, with the use of zoomorphic characters, such as the cute kitten protagonist of *Tamala 2010* (2002, by T.o. L.): drawn with sensual humanoid features, her *kawaii* aspect is associated with the capitalistic commodification of this type of icon.

The Shōjo culture had in fact affirmed the prevalence of transgender icons of various kinds, in many cases distant from the social definition of femininity. Especially loved by women, as already mentioned, these characters were the synthesis of virile energy and womanly emotions, in particular heroine warriors with magical powers. An interesting example is represented by Saya, the protagonist of *Blood: The Last Vampire* (id., 2000) by Kitakubo Hiroyuki—on a subject of Oshii Mamoru. Set in the American base of Yokota during the Vietnam War (an element that suggests the film's political background), in appearance Saya is similar to any Japanese girl, but her task is to eliminate the vampires from the base. Despite the sexual panoply, in particular her fetish school uniform, Saya is de facto asexual, since she lives in a liminal zone between human and vampire, caducity and immortality, different nationalities, femininity and virile energy.

LET'S FIGHT!

A particular and illegal speed race between cars takes place every 5 years in the galaxy in an unspecified future. Koike Takeshi's first twelve minutes of *Redline* (2009*) are devoted to a cruel competition, apparently with no rules, underlining the symbiosis between men and cars in an unbound technological combat. The theme,

---

* The acid graphic inspiration for this peculiar animation—which required seven years of work—comes from some classics such as *Star Wars, Akira,* and largely from *Heavy Metal* style and Moebius' creations.

however, is profoundly Japanese: a sports challenge is equivalent to a fight, happening in a suspended zone between moral extremes. The uninterrupted popularity of animations on sports is often due to successful manga adaptations; the most spoiled author until the 1990s was Adachi Mitsuru, for whom baseball is a trope to portray teenagers during their painful transformation into adults—all paired with a wise use of feelings, and able to attract the female audience as well. In addition to classic sports, martial arts are growing in popularity in animation. Once again, some of the best examples have been directed by Sugii Gisaburō, including the feature films *Nine* (1983) and *Get the World and Go* (*Touch - Sebangō no nai ēsu*, 1986)—both based on Adachi's manga—and *Street Fighter II—The Animated Movie* (1994, from a popular video game*), a blend of kung-fu, wrestling and sumō.

Oshii Mamoru dedicated two live action films to the worlds of video games and virtual fighting—*Avalon* (2001) and *Assault Girls* (2009)—as well as one of his most mature animated works, *Sky Crawlers* (2008, from a novel by Mori Hiroshi). To satisfy the desire for violence in a world that has definitively eliminated wars, the European corporation Lautern and the Japanese Rostock virtually simulate the conflicts through young pilots called Kildren, who battle warily against a virtual sky broadcast by television. The Kildren will never become adults because they are genetically modified to be eternal adolescents until they are killed in battle—they are in a state of suspended existence, symbolizing contemporary Japanese youth, which also suggests the contamination of human identity with synthetic technology.

The virtual parallel dimension is also the theme of a successful animation of 2009, *Summer Wars* (directed by Hosoda Mamoru): young Kenji must face an electronic attack on Oz—a site where millions of people gather through their avatars—that would

---

* Video games are often adapted into animations. The most famous example is *Final Fantasy*, a video game created for Square by Sakiguchi Hironobu. Since 1987, it has been the subject of several films and television remakes.

create an international catastrophe. The plot thus explores many extremes of Japanese society: real and fantastic, economy and utopia, tradition and modernity, individualism and mass culture, and at the same time the widespread fears of technological research.

Regarding the fighters in the scientific contexts, one of the most interesting titles of the new millennium is *Steamboy* (2004), the first animated feature film by Ōtomo Katsuhiro after *Akira*.* In Victorian England, young Ray, grandson of a scientist from whom he inherited a mysterious metal sphere (it turns out to be a steam sphere capable of generating energy), is involved in a series of incredible adventures against the interests of some institutions. The steampunk setting gives a special atmosphere to the challenge, enriched by technological, labyrinth-like details.†

In the same years, *chanbara* and horror genres were still very successful: *The Dagger of Kamui* (Kamui no ken, 1985, by Rintarō) is only one of the many titles on famous heroes of the past, whether *ninjas*—such as *Ninja Scroll* (*Jubei ninpūchō*, 1993, by Kawajiri Yoshiaki) or legendary figures such as Miyamoto Musashi. Also, warriors who fight against demons are very popular, as the mischievous samurai of *Legend of the Millennium Dragon* (*Onigamiden*, 2011, by Kawasaki Hirotsugu) and especially the manga series *Inuyasha* by Takahashi Rumiko (which also appeared in animated versions).

The war theme is frequently revisited in the latest animations, mainly set during the Second World War, in some cases based on well-known stories (such as *The Diary of Anne Frank—Anne no nikki*, 1995, by Nagaoka Akinori); some movies even alter events with nationalist instances, as in the case of *Deep Blue Feet* (*Konpeki no kantai*, 1993, by Kanda Takeyuki and Matano Hiromichi), an

---

* Ōtomo also directed live action movies, including *World Apartment Horror* (1991) and *The Bugmaster* (*Mushishi*, 2008).

† The steampunk atmosphere is recurrent in many animated movies of the last years, including *The Empire of Corpses* (*Shisha no teikoku*, 2015, by Makihara Ryōtarō).

adaptation of Aramaki Yoshio's revisionist work.* Inspired by actual events, one of the best titles is *Giovanni's Island* (*Jobanni no shima*, 2014, by Nishikubo Mizuho), the story of the Soviet occupation on the Japanese island of Shikotan at the end of the Second World War, whose conflict is filtered through the relationship among two Japanese little brothers and the young daughter of the Russian commander in charge of governing the island.

The 1999 feature film *Jin-Roh* (the correct transliteration, jinrō, means wolf men), written by Oshii Mamoru and directed by Okiura Hiroyuki, tells about the consequences of the Second World War and of the subsequent occupation of Japan. In the late 1950s, Fuse Kazuki is a member of a special police unit, known as Kerbero (from Cerberus), committed to counteract the actions of a group of terrorists. One day, Fuse meets a girl who pretends to be the sister of a terrorist who had died during an attack; however, she is actually part of a plot. Based on the metaphor of a kind of Little Red Riding Hood—a tale also narrated in the film—the plot offers many indications of the moral disorder of the period and of human responsibilities in the political management of individuals. Above all, as Oshii pointed out, this story describes the relationship between a man and the beast that lives inside him, resembling Japan in a time of peace, when various tensions lie in a pit of intrigue.

As we are going to see in the next pages, in *Princess Mononoke* (*Mononoke hime*, 1997, by Miyazaki Hayao), wolves are animals of a particular mythological value: the Japanese considered them to be messengers of gods and protectors of nature, and for the ethnic minority Ainu, they even represented ancestors. In *Jin-Roh* and in many animations of the last decades,† this animal has often been chosen as a symbol of freedom. This is also the theme of

---

* Different is the case of other animations such as *In This Corner of the World* (*Kono sekai no katatsumi ni,* 2016, by Katabuchi Sunao), set during the same conflict, for which the staff conducted detailed research to verify the historical truthfulness of the events. It won the Ōfuji Noburō Award Prize that same year.

† For an analysis of the wolf figure (and dog) in *manga* and animation, see Levi, 2006.

two feature films: *One Stormy Night* (*Arashi no yoru ni*, 2005), adapted by Sugii Gisaburō from the work by Kimura Yūichi, and *Wolf Children* (*Ookami no kodomo no Ame to Yuki*, 2013) by Hosoda Mamoru. The first movie tells of the difficult friendship between a wolf and a lamb, strongly opposed by the wolf pack and the flock; the second film narrates the story of two children, the son and the daughter of a human woman and of a wolf-man, who must choose whether to live as humans or wolves. Hosoda also dealt with a similar theme in his last film *The Boy and the Beast* (*Bakemono no ko*, 2015), in which the relationship between an anthropomorphic beast (in this case, a bear) and a boy becomes the reason for reaching maturity and finding his own true father.

Asura (*Ashura*, 2012, by Satō Keiichi), a good adaptation of George Akiyama's manga published between 1970 and 1971 in *Young Magazine*, probably represents the most extreme example of a wolf-man. In the fifteenth century, Japan is devastated by wars and famines; a woman gives birth to a child, who survives despite living in isolation and grows like a semi-wolf in the wild, killing animals and people along his path to eat them. Only an encounter with a monk before and with a kind girl later will make a small spark of humanity emerge in him. Made with hybrid animation—animated computer graphic characters on watercolor-painted backdrops—at Tōei Animation, its realistic impact emphasizes its strong message: you get used to violence until you feel pain, and the greatest suffering comes from love.

MIND AND MEMORY

Animation is the art that can better shape the complexity of the human mind. In the history of Japanese animated cinema, the flows of thought have often been adapted into various styles. Among the films of the new millennium on the subject, *Mind Game* (2004, from a manga by Nishi Robin) by Yuasa Masaaki, winner of the prestigious Ōfuji Noburō Award Prize among other awards, is a triumph of shapes, styles, film genres and techniques (from traditional mixed animation to computer graphic and rotoscope, among others) on the subject of the vulnerability of the mind. A young man finds himself involved in an assault by two yakuzas and is killed. In the presence of God (represented in an incredible variety of iconic forms and functions), he is given the opportunity to return to Earth and try to be a different man. The film opens and closes with a similar tight sequence of scenes from the life of the characters, embedded in a seemingly incoherent flow, meanwhile demonstrating with the various events the differences that arise from a different mental approach.

In Japan, the post-bubble economic crisis of the 1990s had stimulated the production of psycho-horror movies, a genre suitable to translate social anxiety and to shape, albeit allegorically, various deviations arising from insecurity. Animation movies, that is, live actions, often describe the state of solipsism of the characters who are torn between excesses of passion and disenchantment of feelings and whose flux of altered consciousness drives them to commit violations or to be victims. Many examples of alterations are often related to those provided by extrasensory perceptions, such as with mediums or those who live in the paranormal world.* Emotional fractures and fears are often represented as an inexhaustible mental labyrinth. Again, the titles are many, often with grotesque or sumptuous surroundings and rich symbols, as in the successful short film *Kakurenbo: Hide and Seek* (2004) by Morita Shūhei, where a group of children goes on an adventure to the city of demons and disappears, with the exception of the leading character destined to become a demon himself.

Among the mental processes, memory is often used in all possible variants: violated, re-elaborated, exploited or fetishistically approached. For example, memory is the protagonist of the 2001 surreal short film *Cat Soup* (*Nekojiru sō*, inspired by Nekojiru's

---

* Among the various movies, in 1996 Rintarō adapted one of the most controversial works by CLAMP, *X/1999*. With a larger dose of occult components, see the Nippo-Russian co-production *First Squad* (2009, by Ashino Yoshiharu, Aljosha Klimove and Misha Sprits), set during the Second World War.

work), directed by Satō Tatsuo, with Yuasa Masaaki's screenplay and artistic direction. The film unfolds like an acid trip in a bush of death and horror: a kitten seeks to retrieve the part of its sister's soul that had been stolen by Death and does this by going through various spectra of civilization and many signs of our historical memory, like symbols of apocalyptic wars, scientific horrors and extreme fetishes.

Memory is often assaulted and erased, as in the catastrophic *A Wind Named Amnesia* (*Kaze no na wa amneshia*, 1990, by Rintarō), where almost all humanity loses its memory because of a mysterious wind, or in the most interesting experiment *Interstella 5555* (ibid., 2003, by Matsumoto Leiji and Takenouchi Kazuhisa), completely based on the music of the techno-pop group Daft Punk, where four blue-skinned aliens are kidnapped while performing in a concert on their planet and wiped of their memories.

Memory sometimes is a dangerous mechanism that nostalgically binds us to the past, isolating us from real life. It is the theme of one of the most successful animated anthologies of the 1990s, a project by Ōtomo Katsuhiro entitled *Memories* (1995), in particular the first episode, *Magnetic Rose* (*Kanojo no omoide*, by Morimoto Kōji*). Two astronauts exploring galactic debris discover a mysterious structure containing a fantastic and baroque but fictitious world (hologram-recreated environments, objects that crumble to the touch): it is the empty dimension created by the mind of a woman, a sort of sybil who attracts into her past anyone who enters her space, transforming them into actors of her own virtual existence. This is not surprising, considering that this episode is based on the script and has the artistic direction of Kon Satoshi, one of the greatest poets of dream, mind and memory.

---

* The other two episodes are entitled *Stink Bomb* (*Saishū heiki*) and *Cannon Fodder* (*Taihō no machi*), directed by Okamura Tensai and Ōtomo Katsuhiro, respectively.

OBJECTIVE AND SUBJECTIVE REALITY: THE CINEMA OF KON SATOSHI

Tragically deceased in 2010 when he was only forty-seven years old, Kon Satoshi had not only been one of the most brilliant Japanese animators but also one of the most complete filmmakers in the history of international cinema. Kon approached the world of images when he was very young, dreaming of becoming a painter and enrolling in the visual communication design department of the Musashino Art University.* In 1984, he won the Chiba Tetsuya prize for debuting cartoonists promoted by *Young Magazine* with the manga *Toriko*, and in the following year, while he was still a student, he joined the magazine. In the same year, he began his collaboration with Ōtomo Katsuhiro, writing the story and making the drawings for the manga *World Apartment Horror* (1990) and the screenplay for the live action movie version that Ōtomo directed in 1991. The next animated production by Ōtomo, *Rōjin Z* (1991), was directed by Kitakubo Hiroyuki with artistic supervision by Kon.

From this moment on, Kon's path to animation and manga ascended: a collaboration for the layouts of *Run, Melos!* (*Hashire, Merosu*, 1991, by Ōsumi Masaaki from a work by Dazai Osamu), the artistic encounter with Oshii Mamoru in 1993 with *Patlabor 2* (again as curators of the layouts), the direction of the fifth episode in the OVA series *Jojo's Bizarre Adventure* (*Jojo no kimyōna bōken*, 1993), and then the experience in *Magnetic Rose*. At the same time, he published many manga series, including *Opus* (1995–1996) and *Seraphim—266,613,336 Wings* (*Serafimu: 2 oku 6661 man 3336 no tsubasa*, in collaboration with Oshii Mamoru).

In 1997, he made his first animated feature film, *Perfect Blue,*† produced by Madhouse, as were all Kon's future works. The young singer Mima decides to leave her successful band to pursue

---

* The biographical information about this director is taken from his blog at http://konstone.s-kon.net/modules/works/index.php?content_id=1.
† Freely adapted from the 1991 novel by Yoshikazu Takeuchi. The same subject was adapted into a film in 2002 with the same title by Satō Toshiki.

a career as an actress in the psycho-drama "Double Bind," but since a stalker draws her name in an online diary—along with a series of mysterious deaths in her work entourage—Mima's mental stability gradually alters and she believes that she has become a schizophrenic. It tells of the constant osmosis between narrative plans, intended to pilot the *tourbillon* of madness on the thread of an illusory line between imagination and the real world. The background of Mima's identity is performed through a dense film grammar based on flashbacks, oneiric images, film in the film strategies and complex editing techniques that continuously mislead narrative coherence. References to black chronicle episodes and to famous movies such as Hitchcock's *Vertigo* reinforce the objectivity of the narrative as well as a detailed and realistic description of the environments.

Kon's second film, *Millennium Actress* (*Sennen joyū*, 2001*), once again confirms his talent and preference for female portraits, as well as his ability to explore the liminal areas of both reality and idealism. Filmmaker Tachibana decides to shoot a documentary about the elderly Fujiwara Chiyoko, once the greatest star of Gin'ei Studios. The woman's memories, swirling between her own existence and the plots of the films she acted in, cross almost a century of images and events of real society. Here again, the film becomes an homage to the entire world of cinema, not only because it is rich in film quotes referring to Japanese masterpieces from the 1930s to the 1960s,[†] inspired mainly by the actresses Hara Setsuko and Takamine Hideko, who had been protagonists of those years, but also, in particular, in its capacity as the seventh art to replicate the real world in a plausible game of entanglement and deception.

---

* A book was published as an adaptation of the film: *Kon's Tone: The Road to Millennium Actress* (*Kon's Tone: Sennen joyū e no michi*), Tokyo, Shōbunsha, 2002.
† The main reference seems to refer to a three-part colossal film directed by Ōba Hideo between 1953 and 1954: *What is Your Name?* (*Kimi no na wa*), based on a successful radio drama. It tells about the love story between two young people who meet on a bridge during an aerial incursion and promise to meet again on the same bridge six months later, forgetting to exchange their names.

The following feature film is inspired by John Ford's *The Three Godfathers* (1948). *Tokyo Godfathers* (2003) tells the story of three beggars who find an infant abandoned in the trash on Christmas Eve. Initially uncertain whether to give it to the police or not, they decide to trace his parents to understand why they had abandoned him, and in their search, they incur a series of adventures. All three of them seem to have a dual existence, as they belong to a dilated present, without perspectives for the future, and to a hidden past, not entirely left behind. Once again, Kon does not hide his love for cinema, especially through the numerous gags shot in the most classic slapstick style.

Kon's only TV series, *Paranoia Agent* (*Mōsō dairinin*, 2004, 13 episodes)—a work in his simple style, especially for his choice of splitting individuals between reality and fantasy—is followed in 2006 by his last feature film *Paprika* (based on a science fiction novel by Tsutsui Yasutaka). Scientist Chiba Atsuko and her colleague have developed some prototypes of the DC-Mini, a machine that allows one to penetrate into people's dreams. When some of the devices are stolen, Atsuko herself uses it (by means of her alter ego Paprika) for her investigation. Meanwhile, all dreams and hallucinations blend together, flowing into an oneiric dimension in a parade of icons of human obsessions (symbols of consumerism, animals, mythological and religious characters). Many of the signs of Kon's world are once again used in this new title, including the splitting of Atsuko with her alter ego Paprika and real life that blends into dreams, producing an imaginary whim.

In a joint project of several production companies, including NHK and Madhouse, in 2008 *Ani*kuri 15* (meaning animation and creator) was presented. It was a short film composed of fifteen episodes shot by different directors, including Oshii Mamoru, Shinkai Makoto and Kon, who were asked to interpret in their own way what people are able to perceive within sixty seconds. Kon's short animation, entitled *Good Morning* (*Ohayō*), plays on the same concept of splitting the perception of reality in the first moment of a woman's ordinary day.

Kon's next project was supposed to have been a work entitled *The Dream Machine* (*Yume miru kikai*), which was intended as a story set in the future and aimed at children, an attempt inspired by Tezuka Osamu's classic animation. Unfortunately, the director's illness stalled its production. Kon was aware that he had arrived at the end of his life and chose his blog to publish a message entitled *Goodbye* (*Sayōnara*): "With my heart full of gratitude for everything that is good in the world, I will put down my pen. Sorry, now I have to go."*

---

* http://konstone.s-kon.net/modules/notebook/archives/565.

CHAPTER 6

"Alone, Not Lonely": Generation X

ACCORDING TO THE ANNUAL report drawn up by the Japanese Animation Association (*Nihon dōga kyōkai*), since 2010, Japan's lively production industry, with 87% of its studios headquartered in Tokyo, has been rapidly expanding, especially due to the spread of new media and the opening of larger global markets.* In 2016, there was also a significant reversal trend: animations for adults (considered for evening programs) for the first time numerically exceeded those for children and families (for daytime programs). Another important point suggested by the association is the speed with which the titles climb the charts, to the point that Shinkai Makoto's latest success, *Your Name* (*Kimi no na wa*, 2016), took only twenty-eight days to earn the same income as *Princess Mononoke* (*Mononoke hime*, Miyazaki Hayao's record at the box office) did in 1997; however, in the latter case, the same amount was reached four months after its release.

---

* In 2015, a 178.7% increase has been estimated in the sale of rights for the Chinese web market alone. Source: Annual Report of the Association, available in Japanese at http://aja.gr.jp/jigyou/chousa/sangyo_toukei.

In international distribution, the names of some directors prevail over many others—especially those of Miyazaki Hayao, Takahata Isao, Kon Satoshi, Hosoda Mamoru, Oshii Mamoru, Ōtomo Katsuhiro and Shinkai Makoto—whose movies have also been distributed through the home video market in many countries. However, if we exclude rare screenings in festivals, the vast majority of independent animation, mostly experimental, is largely overshadowed in the West. Their authors, almost all beginning careers in Tokyo, are exploring every possible form of artistic expression, often taking charge of the production and promotion of their works. Despite the variety of styles, a leitmotiv seems to consist of their refusal to refer to the tradition of *anime*, which is so popular in the Western world, especially the works produced by the renowned Studio Ghibli.

THE BIRTH OF STUDIO GHIBLI: MIYAZAKI HAYAO AND TAKAHATA ISAO

The collaboration between Takahata Isao and Miyazaki Hayao dates back to the 1960s, when they were both working for Tōei. They later moved to A Production, founded by Ōtsuka Yasuo, where they collaborated—among the various animations—on the making of *Panda! Go Panda!* (*Panda kopanda*, 1972). In 1973, they began work at Zuiyo Eizō, where they produced many television series based on the most successful international literature, as in the case of the aforementioned *Heidi*. Thanks to their cooperation, Miyazaki directed his first feature film, *Lupin III—The Castle of Cagliostro*. Despite the low budget, the film stood out for the accurate details and stylistic richness of European matrix environments, as well as for the general absence of erotic and violent aspects that appeared more pronounced in other adaptations. Well-calibrated among its comic and thriller components, it proved to be a success and confirmed Miyazaki's name in the pantheon of Japanese animators, making him also earn the Ōfuji Noburō Award.

Nausicaä of the Valley of the Wind,* the next film by Miyazaki, was based on the first of the sixteen episodes of his manga and counted on the support of Takahata as a producer. Set in a far post-apocalyptic future, the protagonist Nausicaä,† daughter of the King of the Valley, is an able but pacifist warrior who has to face the destruction of her planet because of a war between two neighboring nations, at the same time trying to explore the nearby Toxic Jungle. The whole story is narrated through many symbols from mythology and the history of Japan and the West. Some of the characteristics of Miyazaki's next works and of their utopian worlds are already present in this film: a narration without excessive erotic or violent nuances; the choice of a clever, strong, and brave female protagonist; and the solemn (and at the same time enthusiastic) music score by composer Joe Hisaishi. In addition, a great deal of attention is given to the description of nature and technological tools, midway between futuristic and medieval. Finally, the theme of flying, in this case, that of Nausicaä riding her glider Mehve. Miyazaki's enchanted world is not based in Manichean dualism; his heroines demonstrate that evil is a human creation, since there are positive components in everyone that can be highlighted through respect, solidarity and tolerance.

Given the success of this film, the two animators, together with Tokuma's president (Tokuma Yasuyoshi), decided to launch a new production business for art animations, free from commercial concerns, and in 1985, Studio Ghibli was founded.‡ The first

---

* The series continued until 1994. This film was also awarded the Ōfuji Noburō Award.
† The character of Nausicaä is inspired by the legendary figure of the Princess of the Feats, who saves Ulysses from the shipwreck in the Odyssey, and also by the protagonist of an ancient Japanese tale, *The Princess Who Loved Insects* (*Mushi mezuru himegimi*) from the twelfth century collection *Tales of the Riverside Middle Counselor* (*Tsutsumi chūnagon monogatari*).
‡ The name refers to the wind of the Sahara Desert—a symbol of a warm air on the world of animation—and also to the codename of the Caproni Ca. 309 airplane used in Africa during the Second World War, among Miyazaki's favorites. His father and uncle were the heads of Miyazaki Airplanes, the company that produced the famous Zero fighters during the Second World War.

film, directed by Miyazaki and set between the nineteenth and twentieth centuries, was *Castle in the Sky* (*Tenkū no shiro Rapyuta*, 1986*). Young Sheeta is fleeing from a group of pirates who are attacking the airplane on which she is traveling; she reaches a village and lands—thanks to the power of the mysterious pendant of her necklace—in a boy's arms. The young man helps her find her homeland, Laputa, a floating island in the sky that everyone ignores. The settings are inspired by the Welsh countryside and mining areas, where Miyazaki had previously traveled to look for the ideal location. The adventures of the two young orphans reflect their evolution toward adulthood through a very personal conquest of freedom. As in other works by Miyazaki, flight and technological inventions are among his main themes.

In 1988, two titles were produced at Studio Ghibli: *My Neighbor Totoro* (*Tonari no Totoro*†) by Miyazaki and Takahata's *Grave of the Fireflies* (*Hotaru no haka*). The first film features two little sisters who have just moved to the countryside with their father to be closer to their hospitalized mother. In the new home and in the surrounding grove, they come in contact with some supernatural entities, especially the sweet Totoro,‡ which, just like a Shinto god, protects them during their adventures. Unlike the author's first features, in this film, the settings are exclusively Japanese,§ representing the ideal place for the appearance of the various *yōkai*, and in particular the great camphor tree that hosts Totoro—with the same sacred function as a Shinto temple. The description of

---

* The title and the adventurous structure of the whole story, including the image of the flying island, are based on Jonathan Swift's *Gulliver's Travels*, although many elements can be traced back to other European classics, such as *Treasure Island* by Robert Louis Stevenson.

† The thirteen-minute spin-off *Mei and the Baby Cat Bus* (*Mei to Konekobasu*) was made in 2001, presented at the Ghibli Studio Museum.

‡ The character of Totoro is inspired by Miyazawa's tale *The Acorns and the Wild Cat*. The Totoro character later became the logo of Studio Ghibli.

§ The film includes many autobiographical references: the locations are the same ones where Miyazaki had lived, and the hospital scenes are inspired by the many years that his mother had spent in the hospital for spinal tuberculosis.

this fantastic world represents a bridge between reality and the most fantastic dimension of childhood and puberty.

Grave of the Fireflies, based on Nosaka Akiyuki's novel of 1969, is set in 1945 and tells the story of orphaned siblings trying to survive during the war in the city of Kobe. The tragedy of their death is revealed in the very first scenes of the film; then, a long flashback describes their escape from the house during an air raid, the loss of their mother, their exploitation by an aunt, and finally their wandering and decay. While Miyazaki's world is mainly fantastic, Takahata prefers realism, thanks to which the heaviest notes of the plot never end in easy pietism, while the complexity of the characters is given by the balanced mix of their feelings.*

Thanks to the first title, the studio launched intense merchandising of various gadgets, and Suzuki Toshio, the former editor of Animage, joined the studio and soon became its director. Productions were planned according to a set of rules: constant attention to marketing, an intense promotion of every movie, and the stipulation of fixed export contracts that were meant to keep the originals unaltered and to diversify production, including advertising and music videos.†

In the following three years, the two animators produced two new titles: Miyazaki's Kiki's Delivery Service (Majo no takkyūbin, 1989) and Takahata's Only Yesterday (Omoide poroporo, lit. Memories Come Tumbling Down, 1991).‡ The first movie tells of a young witch who has to survive for a year away from her home to complete her own magic internship—again, a story about a

---

* In an interview by Animage with both Nosaka Akiyuki and Takahata Isao in 1987, the authors agreed that the story recalls the tragic double suicides (shinjū) theme, so widely present in Japanese past and traditional literature. Published by the magazine Animerica Magazine with the title Takahata and Nosaka: Two grave voices in animation, vol. 2, n. 11, available at the link: http://ghiblicon.blogspot.it/2011/04/animerica-interviews-isao-takahata-and.html.

† Among others, the short video On Your Mark for the Japanese duo Chage & Aska, directed by Miyazaki in 1994.

‡ Based on Kadono Eiko's novel and on Okamoto Hotaru and Tone Yuko's manga, respectively.

girl who builds her identity through an innocent idealism in a world without adversity. The film gained a great audience and critical consensus, demonstrating that it was now necessary to organize production more systematically. Miyazaki announced some important novelties, in particular the solution to cyclically recruit full-time staff members after proper training. Takahata's new film was produced by adopting this new formula and turned out to be a box office success, while Miyazaki's new project *Porco Rosso* (*Kurenai no buta*, 1992) was starting to take shape.

Only Yesterday, a further opportunity for Takahata to bring his realism to perfection retraces the main stages of a woman's growth, alternating moments of her current life in 1982 to flashbacks of her childhood in 1966. Miyazaki's *Porco Rosso*[*] is based on his own manga and soon became a hit. Along with the recent *The Wind Rises* (*Kaze tachinu*, 2013), this film is the most reminiscent of Miyazaki's passion for flights. Now ready for large-scale production, in 1993, Studio Ghibli for the first time inaugurated a series of titles that were not directed by the Takahata-Miyazaki duo. The first one was *Ocean Waves* (*Umi ga kikoeru*), a light comedy by Mochizuki Tomomi. The most interesting among the young filmmakers was Kondō Yoshifumi, who debuted at Studio Ghibli with the delightful *Whisper of the Heart* (*Mimi o sumaseba*, 1995[†]), unfortunately his only movie, since he died of an aneurysm in 1998.

In 1994, Takahata presented his new *Pon Poko* (*Heisei tanuki gassen Ponpoko*, lit. *Heisei-Era Raccoon Dog War Ponpoko*[‡]).

---

[*] The initial project was to make a short film to be screened on board Japan Airlines airplanes. Set in Italy in 1929, the story is about an aviation pilot who is totally nauseated by the Fascist power grip and decides that he no longer wishes to be a man, turning his appearance into that of a pig and choosing to live as a mercenary by hunting for pirates in the sky over the Adriatic Sea.

[†] Written by Miyazaki from a manga by Hiragi Aoi, the film tells of the 14-year-old Shizuku and of her encounter with a mysterious boy.

[‡] The onomatopoeic word *ponpoko* indicates the classic drumming that the *tanukis* perform on their belly or on their testicles. They are protagonists of the film, busy to use their transformation powers to oppose the urbanization of the area around the river Tama, a project that had already started in 1966.

Here again, the author included the ecological subtext that characterizes the studio's production, enriched by a dense net of references to the spheres of art, religion and mythology. They are very well represented by the same *tanukis*, different in appearance,* depending on the context in which they are portrayed and on the comic or dramatic role that they perform.

Princess Mononoke, the eleventh feature film of Studio Ghibli, was released in 1997 and proved to be a great hit. It was awarded several prizes and was selected to represent Japan at the Oscars. Despite the abundant use of computer graphics, already experienced in *Pon Poko*, it took three years to complete this touching historical drama set in the Muromachi period. It tells the story of young Ashitaka, who is attacked and infected by a boar god and destined to die, unless he finds the god-deer able to heal his wound. He travels to the land of Yamato, where he gets involved in a war engaged between a mysterious girl abandoned by men and bred by wolves, San (or Mononoke, meaning spectrum or supernatural being), and the people of a village of miners headed by the aristocratic Lady Eboshi.† The characteristic themes of ecology, animism and technology in Miyazaki's work again show his positive attitude toward progress and human nature.

Two years later came Takahata's *My Neighbors the Yamadas* (*Hōhokekyo tonari no Yamada kun*, from Ishii Hisaichi's manga), an experimental collage of sketches on the everyday life of a normal Tokyoite family, marked by a division into chapters and described in a style that recalls ancient Japanese sketches and *haiku* poetry.

---

* They are realistic when viewed by men, anthropomorphic bipeds when they are alone in their community, cartoon-style in the funniest scenes—in this case, inspired by Sugiura Shigeru's stripes—and humans with dark eyes when they blend among people.
† Lady Eboshi is, at the same time, the creator of the struggle against the deities of nature and the protector of the weak of all forms: lepers, pariahs and women otherwise destined to prostitution. Therefore, she does not represent a negative type.

THE *SHŌJOS* OF THE 2000S CONQUER THE WORLD

With the advent of the new millennium, the system regulated by the so-called *seisakuiinkai** ("production committees"), which had appeared in the 1980s, started to be gradually imposed on the Japanese media industry. It was all about different companies sharing the production costs of a project and taking charge of the local and international distribution through a mix of different media strategies. This system not only allowed the best possible sponsorship with minimal investments, for example, by distributing a project on different platforms (cinema, manga, video games, publishing, merchandising and music media), but it also significantly reduced the risk of competition within the sectors and contrasted with the increasingly emerging web platform. As of today, and in the case of the major productions, a massive temporary recruitment of entertainers and operators belonging to this sector is taking place in areas outside Japan, such as South Korea. Through this system, large companies benefit from extreme flexibility, while individual operators or small companies can acquire methodologies and technologies and thus attempt a productive improvement. This is how many famous films such as *Ghost in the Shell 2*, coproduced among others by Studio Ghibli, were born.

In the field of animation, one of the first examples of *seisakuiinkai* was *Nausicäa of the Valley of the Wind*. In some cases, unlike movies derived from pre-existing television series (defined as *gekijōban*, also called "movie versions;" an example is the mega-hits derived from *Pokemon*†), many authors are making films that adapt original mangas or novels, and often, a different process occurs when animated series, video games and even novels are produced after the movies. As reported by the University of East Anglia, this is what

---

* The *seisakuiinkai* system was recently analyzed by a team of scholars from the School of Film, Television and Media Studies at the University of East Anglia.

† Pokemon are the leading characters of a large media and merchandising market, from Nintendo games to television series, to feature films such as *Pokemon: The First Movie* (id., 1999) Y. Kunihiko (Ed.).

happened in the case of Madhouse's movies, considered high quality and therefore great investments for later productions.

By analyzing the popularity of animated films at the box office, significant differences are noticeable when a new movie by Studio Ghibli is distributed (a phenomenon called the Ghibli effect), especially if the director is Miyazaki Hayao. One of the greatest hits was recorded in 2001 with the release of his *Spirited Away* (*Sen to Chihiro no kamikakushi*, lit. *Sen and Chihiro hidden by the gods*, from a novel by Kashiwaba Sachiko, Grand Prix winner at the Berlin Festival and at the 2003 Oscars for the best animation). The success of the film was also ensured by a massive *seisakuiinkai* operation formed with Studio Ghibli: the distributor Tōhō made a long advertising campaign, in conjunction with Japan's largest advertising company, Dentsū. Nippon Television Network Corporation officially broadcast videos related to the film. Nestle Japan supplied its products with gadgets from the film and then sold them at the Lawson supermarket chain, which in turn became a partner.

The film tells of the adventures of little Chihiro, who, one day, together with her parents, mistakenly ends up in a town inhabited by spirits of various natures, where the witch Yubaba reigns supreme. It is a film full of intersections between different themes: the world of childhood contaminated by adult consumerism, the attention to ecological issues, an osmosis between shintoist elements and other derivatives from the West, and between fantastic and symbolic creatures with references to Western mythologies. Chihiro is also another example of *shōjo*, an icon of a world halfway between reality and imagination, but absolutely devoid of any erotic sign. It is the new feminine ideal, a small adult in the embryonic stage, who has responsibility derived from having weak parents. The success of *Spirited Away* has spurred the production of a very high number of films, with protagonists similar to the little Chihiro. Studio Ghibli produced important titles in this regard, beginning with *The Cat Returns* (*Neko no ongaeshi*, 2002) by Morita Hiroyuki, a sequel to *Whisper of the Heart*.

The success of this formula was confirmed by Miyazaki's next film: *Howl's Moving Castle* (*Hauru no ugoku shiro*, 2004, from Diana Wynne Jones novel, receiving an award at the Venice Film Festival in 2005). It is the story of young Sophie, who is the victim of a spell that transforms her body into that of an old woman. She finds shelter in the moving castle of the fascinating wizard Howl, and through various adventures, she gradually recovers her youth. The passion for flying (especially in the image of Howl, who can transform himself into a kind of bird), the attention to natural settings inspired by the landscapes in Alsace, harmoniously integrated with technological richness, particularly in the characterization of the castle, are all elements typical of Miyazaki's world, with the novelty of a protagonist who is already eighteen and the novelty of time that goes back to her youth. The Ghibli effect soon produced many films with similar solutions, for example, Madhouse's *The Girl Who Leapt Through Time* (*Toki o kakeru shōjo*, 2006, from a novel by Tsutsui Yasutaka) by Hosoda Mamoru, where a high school student acquires the ability to jump over time and can thus modify the small events of her daily life.

It was again Miyazaki to offer new perspectives, this time bringing attention to much younger female protagonists with *Ponyo on the Cliff by the Sea* (*Gake no ue no Ponyo*, 2008, inspired by Nakagawa Rieko's work and a tribute to Andersen's *Little Mermaid*), presented at the Venice Film Festival.* It is a fairy tale about a little fish that escapes from the depths of the abyss in search of adventures, meets the little Sosuke, and manages to transform itself into a little girl—a masterpiece made by 170,000 handmade designs by seventy artists.

The *shōjo* world is still a protagonist of movies. In some cases, it did not produce remarkable works, as in the case of *Mai Miracle* (*Mai Shinko to sennen no mahō*, 2009), shot without much depth by Miyazaki's former collaborator (and emulator), Katabuchi Sunao. In other cases, many interesting elements suggest new perspectives

---

* At the same festival one year later, Madhouse's response to the enchanted world of the smallest protagonists was presented: *Yona Yona Penguin* (by Rintarō), which tells of the adventures of little Coco.

for the genre, as in the computer-generated animation *Oblivion Island: Haruka and the Magic Mirror* (*Hottarake no shima: Haruka to mahō no kagami*, 2009) by Satō Shinsuke. Many films also explore the magical dimensions of young protagonists through mythological symbols, often linked to fundamental values such as love and friendship. Among the many good movies are Okiura Hiroyuki's *A Letter to Momo* (*Momo e no tegami*, 2011)—a successful balance between comedy and drama—and Studio Ghibli's *The Secret World of Arrietty* (*Karigurashi no Arietti*, 2010, directed by Yonebayashi Hiromasa, from the work by Mary Norton).

While Studio Ghibli presented the second movie by Miyazaki Gorō entitled *From Up on Poppy Hill* (*Kokurikozaka kara*, 2011*), his father Miyazaki Hayao was working on his latest title *The Wind Rises*.[†] Based on the manga by Miyazaki released in 2009 (inspired by the novel by Hori Tatsuo), the film starts in 1918, when the young Horikoshi Jirō[‡] uselessly (because of his short sight) dreams of becoming a pilot and ends with him becoming an airplane designer. The film is different from the others by Miyazaki, and the leading character seems to be the author's alter ego, who stubbornly preserves youthful dreams despite the adversities of life. It is no longer a fantasy proscenium for his own aspirations, and the alternation between happiness and pain becomes the true center of the story.

After eight years of work, in 2013, the studio presented the new film by Takahata, *The Tale of the Princess Kaguya* (*Kaguyahime no monogatari*[§]), hand drawn in the pictorial tradition of the best

---

[*] His first work *Tales from Earthsea* (*Gedo senki*, from the novel by Ursula K. Le Guin) was presented at the Venice Film Festival without, however, great critical consensus.

[†] At the Venice Film Festival, in fact, the film was announced as the last by the filmmaker because of Miyazaki's retirement, a possibility already suggested in the past, and also in this case apparently not definitive.

[‡] Horikoshi Jirō (1903–1962) is well-known for designing the famous Mitsubishi A6M Zero hunting airplane; his fame is equalled by that of Italian engineer Gianni Caproni (in the movie featured in the dreams of the protagonist).

[§] Based on the popular tale of the tenth century, *The Tale of the Bamboo Cutter* (*Takogori monogatari*), tells the legend of a little girl found in a bamboo stem and raised by an elderly couple as a princess.

Japanese ink paintings, with simple, minimalist brushstrokes in pastel colors but animated with fluidity and extreme grace. The film suggests many thoughts, including an accusation of materialism and an excessive attachment to earthly things.

The following film, Yonebayashi Hiromasa's *When Marnie Was There* (*Omoide no Mānii*, 2014, based on Joan J. Robinson's novel) shows a new way to propose the theme of young women portrayed in the most delicate moment of their growth, which unfortunately struggles to reach the qualitative level of the other works of the studio. Although in 2014, Suzuki Toshio had announced an indefinite break in Studio Ghibli's animation department, in 2016, the coproduction *The Red Turtle* by Dutchman Michaël Dudok de Wit was presented—a very good film about a ship wreck on an island populated by beautiful animals. It was a new opportunity to explore ecological instances through the symbolism of nature, and in 2017, it was announced that Miyazaki is back to work on a new feature film.

FROM THE NEW WEB PERSPECTIVES TO THE AUTHORIAL ACHIEVEMENT: SHINKAI MAKOTO

The world of Japanese animation has undergone some profound changes in the last few years, opening to the perspectives that are still in progress through increasingly sophisticated technologies. The so-called computer-generated anime (CGA), for example, has reached the highest levels, thanks to the emergence of low-budget software for digital coloration and a particular mixture between 2D images and 3D computer effects. In addition to the usual web-based TV, themed channels such as Bandai Channel and Crunchyroll have multiplied, and movies are also broadcast directly to the web, called Original Net Anime (ONA) —before being distributed on DVD. The same channels are used in many cases to verify the level of audience satisfaction through pilot episodes, as well as to associate individual works with larger projects.

An emblematic case is represented by Yoshiura Yasuhiro's fantasy *Patema Inverted* (*Sakasama no Patema*, 2013), originally distributed as ONA in 2012 in four episodes and then presented as a feature film. In 2014, a UK-based crowdfunding campaign was launched, gathering in a few hours the necessary budget to make a special version of the movie.

It is through web platforms that the video game graphic designer Shinkai Makoto has emerged as one of the most important animators of the last years. He made his first animations (*Other Worlds* (*Tōi sekai*, 1997) and *She and Her Cat* (*Kanojo to kanojo no neko*, 1999)) completely on his own by using his home computer—distributing them through the web. Thanks to the good feedback, Shinkai worked on his first complex work, the already mentioned *Voices of a Distant Star*, becoming successful enough to join the CoMix Wave production company. Accompanied by a professional staff, he completed his first feature film in 2004, *The Place Promised in Our Early Days* (*Kumo no mukō, yakusoku no bassho*), a delicate story of a friendship capable of lasting over time and beyond the historical vicissitudes, and was awarded with prestigious prizes in the world, including the local Mainichi Awards.

International success comes with *5 Cm Per Second* (*Byōsoku 5 senchimētoru*, 2007), a chain of three short films on the themes of love, incommunicability, the innocence lost in the passage to adult age and the pain of distance. The words are only whispered with melancholy; the images enriched by lights; shadows and transparencies fluctuating as in a dance, together with the particular use of color, the delicate and incisive music by Tenmon (habitual composer of Shinkai's work); and the microscopic details, all elegantly composed.

After spending a year in London in 2011, Shinkai presented his new feature film entitled *Children Who Chase Lost Voices* (*Hoshi no ou kodomo*). Shinkai considered this to be his real movie debut. It is, the tale of the underworld journey—and metaphorically of the journey toward maturity—of young Asuna.[*] Together with the usual techniques, Shinkai added a greater emphasis on poetry, a true source of inspiration for narrative, whispered in the most delicate moments. Poetry is also at the center of his following *The Garden of Words* (*Kotonoha no niwa*, 2013),[†] a delicate love story between a teenager and a more mature woman, lived in an atmosphere of poetry.

Shinkai's latest 2016 movie has achieved an incredible success. *Your Name* has not only been record-breaking at its release but has also internationally reinforced the idea that Shinkai stands as Miyazaki's true heir. The story tells of a girl who lives in the countryside, who exchanges her body and experiences with a Tokyoite boy, both in the obsessive search for each other. The wise balance of feelings, the cultural and mythological quotations and the intersections of situations given by destiny all reveal the gradients of the success of this author.

COLLECTIVE PRODUCTIONS AND THE WORK BY MORIMOTO KŌJI

In recent decades, many short films have gained greater visibility, thanks to the collective projects of which they were part, some of them already mentioned in the previous pages. Among the thirty-five filmmakers who had participated in the 2003 film *Winter Days* by Kawamoto Kihachirō—together with the most famous ones, Takahata Isao, Kuri Yōji and Yamamura Kōji—many were young directors known only in niche circuits. Likewise, the *Tōkyō Loop* project produced by Image Forum in 2006 featured prominent names (Kuri and Yamamura Kōji, as well as Furukawa Taku and Tanaami Keiichi) and some of the most interesting young artists of the decade. The fifteen micro-animations that make up *Ani*kuri 15* include experimental essays by

---

[*] It is especially after this movie that the press began to call Shinkai "the new Miyazaki," a director by whom he has often claimed to be influenced.

[†] Meanwhile, he produced commercials and also took part in the *Ani*kuri 15* project; he also produced a short film entitled *Someone's Gaze* (*Dareka no manazashi*) in 2013.

well-entertained authors in mainstream cinema, such as Nakazawa Kazuto, along with beginning and lesser known authors.

There are also several more ambitious and commercially successful collective projects, such as the Japanese–American production *The Animatrix* (2003), inspired by the Wachowski brothers' *The Matrix* saga, which through renowned names (among others, Kawajiri Yoshiaki, Koike Takeshi and Maeda Mahiro) offers an interesting demonstration of different techniques and styles of animation. Likewise, between 2007 and 2008, Studio 4°C proposed another experiment, divided into two parts entitled *Genius Party* and *Genius Party Beyond*, which collected twelve shorts of themes and styles altogether different, starting with the fantastic abstract introduction of Fukushima Atsuko. Finally, Ōtomo Katsuhiro, already in the past years a curator of omnibus projects such as *Memories*, in 2013, presented *Short Peace*, consisting of four shorts introduced by an animation by Morimoto Kōji, including Ōtomo's *Combustible* (*Hi no yōjin*, winner of the Japan Media Arts Festival Awards), harmoniously combining traditional and refined art animation of the Edo period.

In these collective works, one of the most active animators is Morimoto Kōji,* author of some of the most beautiful episodes of both *Animatrix* and *Genius Party* (the first entitled *Beyond* and the second *Dimension Bomb—Jigen Bakudan*). After several mainstream activities and collaborations with Ōtomo Katsuhiro (for *Akira*, *Robot Carnival* in 1987 and especially for *Memories*, where he directed *Magnetic Rose*), in 1991, he presented the feature *Fly! Peek the Whale* (*Tobe! Kujira no pikku*), after which he mainly made only short movies. His style is anti-realistic, highly symbolic and strongly linked to music, with bodies and places metamorphosed and floating in an undefined space, as demonstrated in particular by his music videos. Examples are: the techno song *Extra* (1995, made with software for Mac) by Ishii Ken and Utada Hikaru, *Four-Day*

---

* He was one of the founders of Studio 4°C in 1986, for which he collaborated until 2011, before starting his own independent studio phy Φ.

Weekend (1998, 2D and infographic) by the British Bluetones, the delightful *Survival* (1999) made in only 1 month for the Japanese band Glay, with *Positive Noise* (2010) for System 7.

Among the shorts, *Noiseman Sound Insect* (*Onkyo seimeitai Noiseman*, 1997) is certainly one of the most successful. Produced with mixed 2D and 3D techniques, abstract animation and a surreal visionary—and at times naive—style, tells of a scientist who creates a synthetic creature called Noiseman, capable of eating music waves and of disseminating terror in the city. Music, words and images interact, creating an uninterrupted vortex of almost tactile sensations. Other digital animations follow, including a brief experimentation using shapes, space and perspective in *Hustle! Tokitama* (1998), predominantly made with a Mac computer. Also in 1998, Morimoto started a feature film entitled *Tekkonkinkreet* (based on a manga by Matsumoto Taiyō*); the movie remained unfinished due to a lack of funds, but the short pilot clip still won the Excellence Award in the Digital Art category of the ACA Media Arts Festival.

Morimoto works in many different fields: commercials; television series, including the most recent *18: The Puzzle That Connects to You* (*18: Kimi to tsunagaru pazuru*, 2017); and short videos for the web for collective projects and an interactive manga for the anti-smoking campaign promoted by the French Ministry of Health in 2010.[†] In addition, he was also among the artists who exhibited in the special "Superflat" by Murakami Takashi at the MOCA Gallery in California. In 2005, he announced the production of the feature film *Sachiko*, which has not yet been completed. Most recently, in 2013, he produced animated sequences of the hybrid animation–live action project with director Miyazaki Mitsuyo, entitled *A Better Tomorrow* (2013) and presented at the Cannes Film Festival.

---

[*] The same subject was adapted for Studio 4°C in the 2006 feature film by American filmmaker Michael Arias, the first non-Japanese animator to direct a movie in Japan. He was later also the author of *Harmony* (2016).

[†] Among them, the nonsensical series *The Eternal Family* (*Eikyu kazoku*, 2000), fifty-three episodes lasting thirty seconds each and produced for the NTT Infosphere.

ANIMATION IS A PLAYGROUND FOR ART

Many experimental filmmakers have contributed to making animation a great form of art, beyond market logics. The names to be quoted are obviously very numerous, but in these next pages, only the most well-known in the western world will be mentioned.*

Among the filmmakers, many are women, such as Maya Yoneshō, one of the young proposals in *Winter Days*. Her work has been known since the end of the 1990s, after her studies in England, with a series of shorts including *The Cactus Boy* (*Saboten kun*, 1993), *The Colored Giraffe* (*Momo iro no kirin*, 1995), and the award-winning *Believe in It* (1998), often made through mixing different media. Starting from *Wiener Wuast* (2005), she uses animation of different subjects made as a flipbook with the background of photos of cities (a project in different towns known as *Daumenreise*).

Yokosuka Reiko, also an animator for *Winter Days*, often uses the *sumie* style, with delicate black ink brushes on traditional *washi* paper or soft pastel colors, watercolors and pencils, by which she creates sinuous images that animate fluidly on the screen through soft metamorphoses. From her debut in 1981 with *Illusions* (*Maboroshi*), her experimentation continued uninterrupted, often with the use of digital (from *Number 7*, 1984); in other cases by using unusual materials such as copper sheets perforated to create images with peculiar perspectives (*Alchemy—Renkinjutsu*, 1984); or digital graffiti, by scratching white images from a black background (*Sculpture by the Moon—Tsuki no chōkoku*, 1988). Popular tradition inspires various figures, such as in *Weird Ghost* (*Nanja monja obake*, 1994) and *The Legend of Namahage* (*Namahage no densetsu*, 1999), sometimes mixing a contemporary rhythm

---

* It is necessary at least to mention the names of some of the major artists: Inaba Takuya, Kondō Akino, Gotō Shōji, Seike Mika, Uekusa Wataru, Hayakawa Takahiro, Maruyama Sayaka, Shishido Kojirō, the duo UrumaDelvi, Bōda (Bowda) Katsushi, Kurashige Tetsuji, Seike Mika, Udo Atsuko, Nogami Suwami, Iki Norihiko and the collective Rinpa Eshidan.

(*Movement*, 2005 and *Gaki the Biwa Player*—*Gaki biwa hōshi*, 2005), where music has the power to transform space.[*]

Some animators may debut in the West, thanks to museum installations, such as at the Venice Biennale of Arts, where in 2011, the work of video artist Tabaimo (nom de plume of Tabata Ayako) was presented. She is an artist who redefines several aspects of daily life through various surreal designs and colors, creating a strong link between Japan's tradition and modernity and defining a space that seems to kick humans.[†] The particular stop-motion technique used by Kosemura Mami has brought the artist's name into international art circuits: her approach consists of recreating streams of photographic images (an average of one every hour), so that they look like paintings, such as a still life or images of plants. When they are put together, they seem to parcel the flow of time and contribute to portray the transience of nature.[‡] Another great name is Ishida Takashi, one of the most celebrated and eclectic protagonists of the contemporary scene, who in turn uses the frame-by-frame technique to link his drawings, so that through their movement, space itself seems to become a physical entity. The film *663114* (2011, devoted to the devastating Tōhoku earthquake), given the Ōfuji Noburō Award, introduced its director Hirabayashi Isamu, freelance artist—born as a graphic designer and later also the author of numerous commercials.[§] Many of his titles (*Doron*—2006, *Babin*—2008, *Aramaki*—2009 and

---

[*] Other works include *Gatekeeper* (*Monban*, 2012) and the animation of the delicate *Moving Calendar* (*Ugoku ekoyomi*, 2012, directed by Matsui Masaya).

[†] From *Japanese Kitchen* (*Nippon no daidokoro*, 1999), her installations often include projection on multiple screens placed around the visitors, such as *Japanese Commuter Train* (*Nihon no tsūkin kaisoku*, 2001). Among the recurring themes are the relationship between interior and exterior images—*The House of Ghosts* (*Obake yashiki*, 2003), *Dolefullhouse* (2007)—and the dichotomy between what truly exists and what we perceive of existence (*Tozen*, 2014, *Mekuru meku ru*, 2014).

[‡] Among the many titles, the three videos composing the work *The Flowering Plants of the Four Seasons* (*Shikigusabanazu*, 2004–2006), and those included in her latest exhibition *Pendulum* (2017).

[§] Not all his works are animated: in some, for example, like *Textism* (2003), he uses a mixed technique of animation and live action.

Shikasha—2010) have been screened at the most prestigious film festivals, including Venice, Berlin, Cannes and Locarno.

Nakata Ayaka directs commercials and at the same time independent experimental shorts: the first important achievement came in 2008 with her short *Cornelis*, a unique dance with a single protagonist used to explore the various moods and essence of movement, which is also the subject of the next *Yonalure: Moment to Moment* (2011, codirected by Sakitani Yuki), a poetic tribute to the night and the moon, as well as to memory. The hypnotic sand animated in stop motion by artist Nagata Naomi in the music video *On and On* (2012), a song by the US rock band The Sea and Cake, introduced this artist to international audiences, while at home, she was already appreciated for her music videos—in particular *The Song of Rain* (*Ame no uta*, 2012) and *Pear of Kotarō* (*Nashi no Kotaro*, 2012)— made with different techniques, animation of sand, collage, silhouettes, animated puppets and clay animation. Iimen Masako is also a renowned sand art performer: her particular technique consists of modeling sand, using her hands and a backlit glass plate as a support; her hand movements, fluid as a dance, are shot by a camera, whose output turns into a true art animation work. The animator Shiroki Saori paints her images directly on glass plates, with amazing effects of light and shadows, as evidenced by, among others, her *Woman Who Stole the Fingers* (*Yubi o nusunda onna*, 2010).

The particular technique of eclectic artist Tsuji Naoyuki's is the afterimage—the visual illusory effect that persists after having for long observed an image that disappears—made with charcoal drawings, from which he erases some parts and draws others, resulting in various shades of gray. He draws his characters with very simple traits, making them look innocent, even though the themes are usually very harsh (death, violence and even cannibalism). His main works include *A Feather Stare at the Dark* (*Yami or mitsumeru hane*, 2003, also presented at the Cannes Film Festival), the *Trilogy of the Clouds* (*Mittsu no kumo*, 2003–2005), *Children of Shadows* (*Kage no kodomo*, 2007), *The Place Where We Were* (2008) and *Mountain* (2017).

Katō Kunio won an Oscar for *The House of Small Cubes* in 2009 (*Tsumiki no ie*, 2008). After his debut with *The Apple Incident* (2001), Katō joined the Robot Studio animation team, where he produced all his films: *Fantasy* (2003) dedicated to the fantasies of a girl, with drawings in soft pastel tones, and *Diary of Tortov Roddle* (*Aru tabibito no nikki*, 2004), in electric tones of blue and green and with shapes that remind us of Dalì's art. With *The House of Small Cubes*,* Katō continued to perfect his visual and narrative art, where human nature stands for a territory of calm nostalgia.

Many last-generation animators have attended some of the most prestigious art universities in the capital, in particular Musashino, Tama Geijutsu and Tōkyō Zōkei. However, after the restyling of the prestigious Geidai University in 2008 (Tōkyō Geijutsu Daigaku— Tokyo University of Arts, founded in 1949) and the inauguration of its animation department, the collaboration among artists has been intensifying. Here, among others, filmmakers Itō Yūichi and Yamamura Kōji presently teach animation. In particular, Yamamura Kōji has, in recent years, contributed to the spread and promotion of the independent animation of less widely known directors. Among the various activities, for example, he founded the blog Unknown Animations (Shirarezaru Animation), through which he presents many independent animations of debuting filmmakers. In addition, since 2006, he has played a decisive role in scouting young artists and presenting unknown names in Japan, collaborating with film critic Doi Nobuaki on the creation of the site Animations: Creators and Critics, a valuable source of information about new releases on the independent international scene.

In 2010, Doi, together with animators Mizue Mirai, Wada Atsuhi and Oyama Kei, also founded the Calf label, with the intent to distribute in DVDs independent Japanese animated works that

---

* The story of a man who builds new floors of his home as the water level rises, until one day he swims down to the first level, retracing his life memories.

would hardly find distribution* otherwise. Artists who adhere to the label have different styles. Mizue Mirai mainly uses abstract shapes through which each image generates a subsequent drawing, many individual paintings intersecting each other to recreate a "visual wonder" effect, as evidenced by the two best-known titles *Modern Number 2* (2011, also presented at the Venice Film Festival) and *Wonder* (2014, presented at the Berlin Festival). The idea of movement for Wada Atsushi, who graduated from Geidai, is predominantly based—as his site explains—on the traditional Buddhist concept of *ma* (the "empty"), that is, "the tension produced between the movements," recreated through the reiteration of movements constantly transforming. Among his titles is *The Great Rabbit* (2012, awarded with the Silver Bear at Berlin), a minimalist animation with deep surreal and dystopic effects. Oyama Kei uses a complex weave of drawings, with bodies portrayed in their carnal quintessence, in sometimes harsh and visceral images, to investigate issues such as death, illness, bullying and social malaise; he uses scans of real images (e.g., his own skin), later elaborating them through colors, shadows or deformations. His most famous work is *Hand Soap* (2008), which won awards in 2010 at the Oberhausen and Hiroshima Festivals.

Many important names joined those of the founders, for example, the duo known as Tochka—composed of Nagata Takeshi and Monno Kazue—inventor of a new animation technique called PiKA PiKA, using flashlight animation. It is a particular kind of street art performed in different places they visit, where the artists ask people to express their creative impulses: each one is given a colored light to draw images in the air, which are filmed and then edited in time lapse.

---

* In 2015, Doi also founded New Deer, with the aim of presenting films in theaters, organizing events in the field of festivals and cultural encounters, even producing and coordinating some films. Since 2015, New Deer has organized a new festival entitled Georama, featuring prominent names in the international animated scene, including Bruce Bickford, Don Hertzfeldt and David O'Reilly.

As we have already seen, the connection between animation and music has always been very strong. Among the youngest emerging filmmakers, two animator–musicians have recently entered the scene: Murai Satoshi and Katō Ryū. Murai is a highly refined author, as he demonstrated in his short *Palm* (2011), and especially in the 2009 video music *A Play*, which he made for the band ALT, to which he himself belongs. Katō Ryū creates shapes from his own musical bases by opening fascinating views on the subconscious and human sensations. He started making animations in 2006, and in his first ones especially, including *Calm* (2006) and *Around* (2007), he offered a dreamy and fascinating journey through images rapidly evolving, as paraphrases of a mental flow.

In the field of puppet animation, digital techniques are now common practice, and veteran Itō Yūichi is one of the most prominent names of this art. Besides being a teacher at Geidai University and founder of the Ion Animation Studio, he was one of the animators chosen by Kawamoto for *Winter Days*. Itō has made a lot of films, including shorts (among his first titles, *Mirror Glasses—Hoshimegane*, 1990), television series for NHK (*Knyacki!—Nyakki*, 1995), some music videos, and the awarded movie *Harbor Tale* (2012), the story of a red brick that separates from its building to freely wander and discover the world with the help of a gull. Stop motion animator Murata Tomoyasu, among the participants in the Tōkyō Loop project, uses a peculiar style through which lights and shadows and a delicate abstraction of movements describe a mix of memory and fantasy. Many of his films have won awards, including *Nostalgia* (*Suiren no hito*, 2000) and *The Scarlet Road* (*Shu no michi*, 2002). In addition to other major titles such as *White Road* (*Shiro no michi*, 2003) and *Rainbow of Winter* (*Fuyu no niji*, 2005), he is also the author of music videos, including *Hero* (2002) for the band Mr. Children.

References

Azuma, H., *Otaku: Japan's Database Animals*, Minneapolis, MN, University of Minnesota, 2009.

Baskett, M., *The Attractive Empire: Transnational Film Culture in Imperial Japan*, Honolulu, HI, University of Hawai'i Press, 2008.

Chun, J. M., *A Nation of a Hundred Million Idiots? A Social History of Japanese Television, 1953–1973*, New York, NY, Routledge, 2007.

Dower, J. W., *Embracing Japan in the Wake of World War II Defeat*, New York, NY, W.W. Norton & Company, 2000, p. 272.

Ettinger, B., *Anipages*, 2010. Available at http://www.pelleas.net/aniTOP/index.php/midoriko_bringiton.

Galbraith, P. W., *Moe*: Exploring virtual potential in post-millenial Japan, *Electronic Journal of Contemporary Japanese Studies*, 2009. Available at http://www.japanesestudies.org.uk/articles/2009/Galbraith.html.

Gill, T., Transformational magic: Some Japanese super-heroes and monsters, in *The Worlds of Japanese Popular Culture: Gender, Shifting Boundaries and Global Cultures*, D. P. Martinez (Ed.), Cambridge, UK, Cambridge University Press, 1998, pp. 45–46.

Hagihara, Y., Kyōto ni okeru animēshon, *Core Ethics*, 5, 2009. Available at http://www.ritsumei.ac.jp/acd/gr/gsce/ce/2009/hy01.pdf.

Haraway, D., *Simians, Cyborgs, and Women: The Reinvention of Nature*, New York, NY, Routledge, 1991.

Ivy, M., Formation of mass culture, in *Postwar Japan as History*, A. Gordon (Ed.), Berkeley, CA, University of California Press, 1993, p. 252.

Iwabuchi, K., Postcolonial desire for 'Asia', in *Popular Culture, Globalization and Japan*, M. Allen and R. Sakamoto (Eds.), London, UK, Routledge, 2006, p. 23.

Lamarre, T., Specieism part 1: Translating races into animals in wartime animation, in *Mechademia 3—Limits of the Human*, F. Lunning (Ed.), Minneapolis, MN, University of Minnesota Press, 2008, p. 92.

Levi, A., The werewolf in the crested kimono: The wolf-human dynamic in anime and manga, in *Mechademia 1–Emerging Worlds of Anime and Manga*, F. Lunning (Ed.), Minneapolis, MN, University of Minnesota Press, 2006, pp. 145–160.

Litten, F. S., *On the Earliest (Foreign) Animation Films Shown in Japanese Cinemas*, 2014. Available at http://litten.de/fulltext/nipper.pdf.

Lock, M., *Twice Dead: Organ Transplants and the Reinvention of Death*, Berkeley, CA, University of California Press, 2002.

Makino, M., Rethinking the emergence of the proletarian film league of Japan (Prokino), in *In Praise of Film Studies: Essays in Honor of Makino Mamoru*, A. Gerow and A. M. Normes (Eds.), Bloomington, IN, Trafford, 2006, pp. 15–45.

Monnet, L., Anatomy of permutational desire: Perversion in Hans Bellmer and Oshii Mamoru, in *Mechademia 5–Fanthropologies*, F. Lunning (Ed.), Minneapolis, MN, University of Minnesota Press, 2010, pp. 285–309.

Mori, M., The uncanny valley, *Energy*, 7(4), 33–35, 1970.

Nishijima, N., A history of experimental film in Japan, in *Japanese Experimental Film & Video 1955–1994*, Tokyo, Japan, Image Forum, 1994, pp. 112–113.

Nishijima, N., Film and video notes, in *Japanese Experimental Film & Video 1955–1994*, Tokyo, Japan, Image Forum, 1994, p. 54.

Nornes, M., Fukushima, Y. (Eds.), *The Japan/America Film Wars: World War II Propaganda and Its Cultural Contexts*, Tokyo, Japan, Cinematrix, 1991, p. 230.

Ono, K., *The Japanese Animator Who Lived In Two Worlds*, 1999. Available at http://www.awn.com/mag/issue4.09/4.09pages/onomochinaga.php3.

Salamon, H., Movie attendance of Japanese children and youth, *Japonica Humboldtiana*, 6, 146, 2002. Available at http://edoc.hu-berlin.de/japonica-hu/6/all/6.pdf.

Stojikovic, J., Cultural crossover: Art and film, in *Directory of World Cinema*, J. Berra (Ed.), Bristol, UK, Intellect, 2010, p. 22.

Ueno, C., Collapse of 'Japanese Mothers', in *Contemporary Japanese Thought*, R. F. Calichman (Ed.), New York, NY, Columbia University Press, 2005, p. 251.

Wells, P., *The Animated Bestiary–Animals, Cartoons, and Culture*, New Brunswick, NJ, Rutgers University Press, 2009, pp. 41–43.

Yamaguchi, K. and Watanabe, Y., *Nihon animēshon eiga shi* (*History of Japanese Animation*), Osaka, Japan, Yubunsha, 1977, p. 16.

Zunz, O., Schoppa, L., Iwatari, N. (Eds.), *Social Contracts Under Stress: The Middle Classes of America, Europe, and Japan at the Turn of the Century*, New York, NY, Russell Sage Foundation, 2002, p. 235.

Bibliography

Akita, T., 'Koma' kara 'firumu' e. Manga to manga eiga, Tokyo, Japan, NTT, 2005.

Allen, M., Sakamoto, R. (Eds.), Popular Culture, Globalization and Japan, London, UK, Routledge, 2006.

Anne, A., Permitted and Prohibited Desires: Mothers, Comics, and Censorship in Japan, Boulder, CO, Westview Press, 1996.

Anne, A., Millennial Monsters – Japanese Toys and the Global Imagination, Berkeley, CA, University of California Press, 2006.

Azuma, H., Kontentsu no shisō – manga, anime, raito noberu, Tokyo, Japan, Seidosha, 2007.

Azuma, H., Otaku: Japan's Database Animals, translated by J. E. Abele and S. Kono, Minneapolis, MN, University of Minnesota, 2009.

Baskett, M., The Attractive Empire: Transnational Film Culture in Imperial Japan, Honolulu, HI, University of Hawai'i Press, 2008.

Bendazzi, G., Animation – A World History (3 Volumes), Boca Raton, FL, Taylor & Francis Group, 2015.

Bolton, C., Csicsery-Ronay Jr, I., Tatsumi, T. (Eds.), Robot Ghosts and Wired Dreams: Japanese Science Fiction from Origins to Anime, Minneapolis, MN, University of Minnesota Press, 2007.

Brodericj, M. (Ed.), Hibakusha Cinema – Hiroshima, Nagasaki and the Nuclear Image in Japanese Film, New York, NY, Columbia University Press, 1996.

Brown, S. T. (Ed.), Cinema Anime: Critical Engagements with Japanese Animation, New York, NY, Palgrave Macmillan, 2006.

Calichman, R. F. (Ed.), Contemporary Japanese Thought, New York, NY, Columbia University Press, 2005.

Cavallaro, D., Anime Intersections: Tradition and Innovation in Theme and Technique, Jefferson, NC, McFarland, 2007.

Chun, J. M., A Nation of a Hundred Million Idiots? A Social History of Japanese Television, 1953–1973, New York, NY, Routledge, 2007.

Clements, J., McCarthy, H., *The Anime Encyclopedia. A Guide to Japanese Animation Since 1917*, Berkeley, CA, Stone Bridge Press, 2006.

Craig, T. (Ed.), *Japan Pop! Inside the World of Japanese Popular Culture*, Armonk, NY, Sharpe, 2000.

Dower, J. W., *Embracing Japan in the Wake of World War II Defeat*, New York, NY, W.W. Norton & Company, 2000.

Furniss, M., *Art in Motion: Animation Aesthetics*, London, UK, John Libbey, 1998.

Furuta, H., *'Tetsuwan Atomu' no jidai. Eizō sangyō no kōbō*, Kyoto, Japan, Sekai Shisōsha, 2009.

Galbraith, P. W., *The Otaku Encyclopedia*, Tokyo, Japan, Kōdansha, 2009.

Gravett, P., *Manga – Sixty Years of Japanese Comics*, London, UK, Laurence King Publishing, 2004.

High, P. B., *The Imperial Screen: Japanese Film Culture in the Fifteen Years' War of 1931–1945*, Madison, WI, University of Wisconsin Press, 2003.

Hu, T. G., *Frames of Anime: Culture and Image-Building*, Hong Kong, Hong Kong University Press, 2010.

Ivy, M., *Discourses of the Vanishing: Modernity, Phantasm, Japan*, Chicago, IL, University of Chicago Press, 1995.

Iwabuchi, K., *Recentering Globalization: Popular Culture and Japanese Transnationalism*, Durham, NC, Duke University Press, 2002.

Lamarre, T., *The Anime Machine: A Media Theory of Animation*, Minneapolis, MN, University of Minnesota Press, 2009.

Levi, A., *Samurai from Outer Space: Understanding Japanese Animation*, Chicago, IL, Open Court, 1996.

Levi, A., McHarry, M., Pagliassotti, D., *Boys' Love Manga: Essays on the Sexual Ambiguity and Cross-cultural Fandom of the Genre*, Jefferson, NC, McFarland, 2010.

Lunning, F. (Ed.), *Mechademia 1 – Emerging Worlds of Anime and Manga*, Minneapolis, MN, University of Minnesota Press, 2006.

Lunning, F. (Ed.), *Mechademia 2 – Networks of Desire*, Minneapolis, MN, University of Minnesota Press, 2007.

Lunning, F. (Ed.), *Mechademia 3 – Limits of the Human*, Minneapolis, MN, University of Minnesota Press, 2008.

Lunning, F. (Ed.), *Mechademia 4 – War Time*, Minneapolis, MN, University of Minnesota Press, 2009.

Lunning, F. (Ed.), *Mechademia 5 – Fanthropologies*, Minneapolis, MN, University of Minnesota Press, 2010.

Lunning, F. (Ed.), *Mechademia 6 – User Enhanced*, Minneapolis, MN, University of Minnesota Press, 2011.

Lunning, F. (Ed.), *Mechademia 7 – Lines of Sight*, Minneapolis, MN, University of Minnesota Press, 2012.

Lunning, F. (Ed.), *Mechademia 8 – Tezuka's Manga Life*, Minneapolis, MN, University of Minnesota Press, 2013.

Lunning, F. (Ed.), *Mechademia 9 – Origins*, Minneapolis, MN, University of Minnesota Press, 2014.

Lunning, F. (Ed.), *Mechademia 10 – World Renewal*, Minneapolis, MN, University of Minnesota Press, 2015.

MacWilliams, M. W. (Ed.), *Japanese Visual Culture. Explorations in the World of Manga and Anime*, Armonk, NY, Sharpe, 2008.

Martinez, D. (Ed.), *The Worlds of Japanese Popular Culture – Gender, Shifting Boundaries and Global Cultures*, Cambridge, UK, Cambridge University Press, 1998.

McCarthy, H., *Hayao Miyazaki: Master of Japanese Animation*, Berkeley, CA, Stone Bridge, 2002.

McCarthy, H., *The Art of Osamu Tezuka – God of Manga*, Lewes, UK, Ilex, 2009.

Miyazaki, H., *Starting point 1979–1996*, translated by B. Cary and F. L. Schodt, San Francisco, CA, VIZ Media, 2009.

Napier, S. J., *The Fantastic in Modern Japanese Literature: The Subversion of Modernity*, London, UK, Routledge, 1996.

Napier, S. J., *Anime – From Akira to Howl's Moving Castle*, New York, NY, Palgrave Macmillan, 2005.

Napier, S. J., *From Impressionism to Anime: Japan as Fantasy and Fan Cult in the Mind of the West*, New York, NY, Palgrave Macmillan, 2007.

Nishijima, N. et al., *Japanese Experimental Film & Video 1955–1994*, Tokyo, Japan, Image Forum, 1994.

Nornes, A. M., Fukushima, Y. (Eds.), *The Japan/America Film Wars – World War II Propaganda and Its Cultural Contexts*, Tokyo, Japan, Cinematrix, 1991.

Novielli, M. R., *Animerama – Storia del cinema d'animazione giapponese*, Venice, Italy, Marsilio, 2001.

Onoda Power, N., *God of Comics. Osamu Tezuka and the Creation of Post-World War II Manga*, Jackson, MS, University Press of Mississipi, 2009.

Patten, F., *Watching Anime, Reading Manga: 25 Years of Essays and Reviews*, Berkeley, CA, Stone Bridge Press, 2004.

Ruh, B., *Stray Dog of Anime – The Films of Mamoru Oshii*, New York, NY, Palgrave Macmillan, 2004.

Saito, T., *Beautiful Fighting Girl*, translated by K. Vincent and D. Lawson, Minneapolis, MN, University of Minnesota Press, 2011.

Shapiro, J. F., *Atomic Bomb Cinema – The Apocalyptic Imagination on Film*, London, UK, Routledge, 2002.

Swale, A. D., *Anime Aesthetics: Japanese Animation and the 'Post-Cinematic' Imagination*, New York, NY, Palgrave Macmillan, 2015.

Tatsumi, T., *Full Metal Apache: Transactions between Cyberpunk Japan and Avant-pop America*, Durham, NC, Duke University Press, 2006.

Tsugata, N., *Nihon animēshon no chikara. 85 nen no rekishi o tsuranuku*, Tokyo, Japan, NTT, 2004.

Yamaguchi, K., Watanabe, Y., *Nihon animēshon eiga*, Osaka, Japan, Yūbunsha, 1978.

Yamaguchi, Y., *Nippon no anime*, Tokyo, Japan, Ten Books, 2004.

Yamamura Kōji, K., *Animēshon no sekai o yokosō*, Tokyo, Japan, Iwanami Shinsho, 2006.

Yokota, M., Hu, T. G. (Eds.), *Japanese Animation: East Asian Perspectives*, Hong Kong, Hong Kong University Press, 2014.

Yomota, I., *'Kawaii' ron*, Tokyo, Japan, Chikuma Shinsho, 2006.

Index

Printed in the United States
by Baker & Taylor Publisher Services